*When David
heard that Nabal
was dead, he said, "Praise
be to the L*ORD*, who has upheld
my cause against Nabal for treating
me with contempt. He has kept his
servant from doing wrong and has
brought Nabal's wrongdoing down
on his own head."
Then David sent word to Abigail,
asking her to become his wife. His
servants went to Carmel and said
to Abigail, "David has sent us
to you to take you to become
his wife."*

She bowed down with her face to the ground and said, "I am your servant and am ready to serve you and wash the feet of my lord's servants." Abigail quickly got on a donkey and, attended by her five female servants, went with David's messengers and became his wife.

—1 Samuel 25:1–42 (NIV)

Ordinary Women of the BIBLE

A MOTHER'S SACRIFICE: JOCHEBED'S STORY
THE HEALER'S TOUCH: TIKVA'S STORY
THE ARK BUILDER'S WIFE: ZARAH'S STORY
AN UNLIKELY WITNESS: JOANNA'S STORY
THE LAST DROP OF OIL: ADALIAH'S STORY
A PERILOUS JOURNEY: PHOEBE'S STORY
PURSUED BY A KING: ABIGAIL'S STORY

Ordinary Women of the BIBLE

PURSUED BY A KING
ABIGAIL'S STORY

Elizabeth Adams & Diana Wallis Taylor

Ordinary Women of the Bible is a trademark of Guideposts.

Published by Guideposts
100 Reserve Road, Suite E200
Danbury, CT 06810
Guideposts.org

Copyright © 2020 by Guideposts. All rights reserved.

This book, or parts thereof, may not be reproduced, stored in a retrieval system, or transmitted in any form or by any means, electronic, mechanical, photocopying, recording, or otherwise, without the written permission of the publisher.

This is a work of fiction. While the characters and settings are drawn from scripture references and historical accounts, apart from the actual people, events, and locales that figure into the fiction narrative, all other names, characters, places, and events are the creation of the authors' imaginations or are used fictitiously.

Every attempt has been made to credit the sources of copyrighted material used in this book. If any such acknowledgment has been inadvertently omitted or miscredited, receipt of such information would be appreciated.

Scripture references are from the following sources: *The Holy Bible, King James Version (KJV)*. *The Holy Bible, New International Version (NIV)*. Copyright ©1973, 1978, 1984, 2011 by Biblica, Inc. Used by permission of Zondervan. All rights reserved worldwide. www.zondervan.com. *Holy Bible, New Living Translation*. Copyright © 1996. Used by permission of Tyndale House Publishers, Inc., Wheaton, Illinois 60189. All rights reserved. Scripture quotations marked (CEV) are from the Contemporary English Version Copyright © 1991, 1992, 1995 by American Bible Society. Used by permission. Certain scripture passages are quoted without attribution to correctly reflect how early believers would have interacted with scripture.

Cover and interior design by Müllerhaus

Cover illustration by Brian Call and nonfiction illustrations by Nathalie Beauvois, both represented by Illustration Online LLC.

Typeset by Aptara, Inc.

ISBN 978-1-961126-59-6 (hardcover)
ISBN 978-1-951015-38-1 (epub)

Printed and bound in the United States of America
10 9 8 7 6 5 4

CHAPTER ONE

Abigail enjoyed the feeling of the sun on her skin as she walked to the marketplace. After so many weeks indoors, she relished its warmth.

Anna quickened her steps to keep up. "Mistress, you must slow down. You need to be careful of your health."

"I feel fine." Abigail stepped to the side to allow a woman trailed by small children to pass. "The fever has gone."

"But you do not yet have your strength back."

Abigail knew she should be grateful for Anna's fretting. Her maid was loyal and kind, and Abigail didn't know what she would do without her. And Abigail knew Anna had been right to be worried. She had just fought off the same fever that had taken her mother several years ago, and she was not back to her full strength. But sometimes Anna needed to simply trust that Abigail knew her own mind.

"I am hoping to find a nice fish for Abba's supper." Abigail tried to distract her. "You are so good at selecting the best choices, so I will value your help in deciding."

The words seemed to placate Anna, who straightened up a bit as she fell into step behind her mistress. Abigail needed tonight's dinner to go well. She had thought of her plan as she lay on her mat so many nights, fighting the fever, and tonight she hoped to make it happen.

"Let's look at the vegetables," Anna said, gesturing at the stalls piled high with squash and cucumbers and greens. She selected some squash, since they had already eaten their own from the garden. They threaded through the narrow alleys, past merchants calling out about the wonders of their lentils and cooking pots and rugs. It was hot and dusty and loud, with too many colors and sights and sounds all fighting for her attention. Abigail loved it.

She looked around for the rug merchant's son, but she did not see him at his family's stall. She had first noticed Ira many months back, during the rainy season, and had approached the stall, pretending she was in need of a rug, to get a closer look. He was a few years older than she, and very handsome. And he had been kind, and his voice deep and rich, as he showed her the many fine rugs on offer. She suspected he had known she wasn't really looking for a rug, and when she had turned to go, he had urged her to come back and see the new rugs they would have the next week. She had come again the next week and the week after that, and even when she could not stop to see his wares, she had met his eye across the marketplace many times. It always sent a surge of excitement through her. But he was not there today. She had not been to market in several weeks. Had something happened to him in that time?

At the spice dealers', she purchased some capers to go with mint from their garden, as well as costly saffron. From the grain merchant, she bought millet and walnuts. For dessert she bought honey and pomegranates for one of her father's favorite desserts, pomegranate and poached apricots in honey syrup.

"Mistress, do you know that man?"

"Who?" Abigail had just placed the fruit in a bag and handed it to Anna, and she looked up to see who Anna was talking about.

"That man over there." Anna was looking across the crowded market to a group of men standing in the shade of the covered portico. A woman led a mule piled with wares past, blocking their view of the men for a moment.

"I do not see who you mean."

"The tall one in the middle there. He keeps looking at you." The woman and the mule passed, and the men came into view again. "I saw him when we were looking at the spices, and here he is again. He is watching you."

Abigail saw who her maid meant now. He was looking right at her. He was handsome, in a rough way, with his dark beard and hair that curled to his shoulders. He was well dressed—a man of means—and she guessed him to be many years older than she was. She had not seen him before. Still looking at her, the man spoke to the merchant in the stall next to him and then nodded his head. He inclined his head toward her, a hint of a smile curving his lips.

Abigail turned and started to thread her way through the crowded alleyway once again. "I do not know him." Something about the way he was looking at her made her uneasy. They continued on past the merchants selling richly dyed fabrics and heaping piles of grains, but she could still feel his eyes on her. She glanced back and saw that he was still looking her way. "Let us go, Anna. I am more tired than I thought."

Anna shook her head but did not say that she'd warned her. Abigail led them through the crowded marketplace, back past the rug merchant's stall once again. Ira was still not there, and she felt a pang of disappointment.

No matter. It would not change her plans for this evening. As they passed a fruit merchant's stall, Abigail saw a small hand dart out and grab a few figs. It did not register as strange until the booming voice of the merchant rang out.

"Stop!"

Abigail saw the small boy trying to run past her, but the man from the next stall, the man who sold olive oil in earthenware jugs, grabbed the boy by his cloak and held him.

"Give back the figs," the fruit seller said. His face was twisted up in anger.

Abigail saw it then. The boy was trembling, and so thin his clothes hung off him. He was hungry. And though she knew she should not do it, though she heard her father's voice begging her to keep her tongue and think before she acted, she could not stop the words that came out.

"Thank you, Ira." It was the first name that came to mind, and she flushed, hoping no one would figure out why. But she went on. "You got the figs I requested. Let me see them."

The boy looked up at her with wide eyes. She nodded at him, silently urging him to play along, and slowly he uncurled his fingers. The fruit seller shifted his feet, watching, but his face still wore a scowl. Anna stood a few paces away, and Abigail recognized the look in her eye. She was silently begging Abigail to walk away before she got herself in trouble. Loyal Anna. Abigail turned back to the boy.

"You have chosen well. Those will go nicely with Abba's meal." She looked up at the fruit seller, a wide smile on her face. "How much do I owe?"

The fruit seller looked from her to the boy and back again. He did not believe her, that much was clear. But he dared not contradict her either. Slowly, seemingly unsure of what to do, he named a price. It was ludicrously high, at least three times what the figs were worth, but Abigail did not flinch. She reached into her dress and pulled her small bag of coins from it, and handed them over. The fruit seller continued to watch her warily, but the other man let go of the boy's clothing.

"Next time, you must tell the man I am coming with payment before you leave the stall," she said to the boy, extending the farce. He nodded, his eyes still wide. "Come," she said, her voice cheerful. "Let us continue on."

The boy followed, still clutching the figs, until they were out of sight of the fruit merchant. Then Abigail stopped and turned to the boy.

"You are hungry."

He nodded.

"How many of you are there?"

"I have three younger sisters." His voice came out quietly, faltering.

"Where is your mother?"

"The fever took her."

The words hit Abigail hard. She bit her lip, looking up at the clear blue sky. Then, when she had calmed herself enough to speak, she said, "I am sorry to hear it."

She gestured for Anna to hand her the bag, and reluctantly, her servant did. Abigail reached in and pulled out the fruit she had purchased for her father's supper, as well as the fish, wrapped in cloth, and the honey and walnuts.

"Take these," she said. "For your sisters."

The boy did not argue. He was probably too hungry to think of it. "Thank you."

"You know how to cook it?"

He nodded.

"Good." Abigail gazed around. She did not see the fruit merchant anywhere, but she did not believe the boy was safe here. "Now, go. You must leave this place before those men find you."

He ducked his head and turned, and in a few moments he had vanished into the crowd. Abigail turned back to Anna.

"It appears we will need to do our shopping all over again."

Anna did not say anything for a moment. Her lips were pursed. Abigail knew she did not approve of what had just happened. Anna was good, true, loyal. She followed the rules to the letter. She was much like Abigail's father in that way. Beyond that, she worried about Abigail. Anna loved her like her own child and had been with her Abigail's whole life. She did not approve of anything that put Abigail in harm's way. But now Anna simply followed Abigail, walking behind her as she returned to the same stalls she had visited shortly before.

It was not until they were back on the road walking toward home that Anna spoke.

"That was foolish, mistress. Anything could have happened to you."

"He was hungry. It would have been cruel not to help him."

"He was getting the punishment he deserved. It is not your place to feed all the thieves and liars in the market."

"He is a *child*, Anna. A child with no mother, and many sisters to feed."

"Still. It is not your place. You must learn to think before you act."

Abigail knew she would get nowhere with her maid, so she let the conversation drop. But she continued the discussion inside her own mind. If it wasn't her place to help, whose place was it? Hadn't Yahweh commanded them to not glean the edges of the fields but leave some for the poor? What was that if not a command to care about those too poor to feed themselves?

As they walked, their feet stirring up fine red dust, she shifted her thinking to what she would say to her father over dinner tonight. She had mentioned Ira to her father several times, speaking of his kindness and the way he made her laugh, so he knew who Ira was. The rug maker's family was in good standing in the village. She was of marriageable age, she would remind him. Many of the girls she had known as a child were already married, and some even had children of their own. It was time for her father to arrange a betrothal for her, she would insist. And Ira was kind and from a good family. His father did well in business. He was also funny, and the way he smiled at her made her stomach feel warm. Tonight she would feed her father well, and after he had had some wine and was feeling relaxed, she would suggest that Ira would make a good husband.

Their steward, Remiel, met them at the door when they arrived home, and he took the items she had purchased from her.

"It is well you have returned, mistress," Remiel said. There was an expression on his face that she couldn't read. "We have a guest, and your father has been anxious to speak with you."

Abigail handed her mantle to Anna and straightened her veil. Was it Ira? Was this why he had not been in the market? She pinched her cheeks to give them color and then walked to the main room that overlooked the courtyard. When she saw him, she stopped suddenly and took a quick breath. The man standing next to her father was not Ira. It was the man from the marketplace. The one who had been watching her.

"Daughter, we have been anxious for your return. You must meet our guest."

Abba put his arm around her shoulders. "Abigail, this is Nabal. He is someone I have known for some time. He is from Maon."

Nabal nodded to her. "If you will forgive me, I was quite taken with you in the marketplace and learned you were the daughter of someone I have done business with for many years. He is a most fortunate man to have such a beautiful daughter."

Abigail felt uneasy with his praise. Why was he here? She smiled briefly, acknowledging his words, but remained silent, looking to her father and then the stranger. Abigail's father was in the business of wool. What did this man have to do with that?

"It is nice to meet you," she said. And then she quickly continued, "Please excuse me. I must speak with the cook and then prepare myself for our evening meal. Will you be joining us?"

"Most assuredly. Your father has kindly invited me to remain for the night. I must return to my estate in Maon in the morning."

An estate? He was indeed a man of means, then. She bowed her head and walked to the room at the back of the house to speak to the cook. She tried to hide her disappointment. She could not speak to her father about Ira if this man was here. Tonight's special meal would be a waste.

Several hours later, they sat on the mats and enjoyed the richly prepared meal: grilled fish drizzled with olive oil, squash with capers and mint, saffroned millet with raisins and walnuts, and fresh bread with goat cheese. Nabal praised the meal and spoke to her father of his fertile land and his success with his herd. He looked at Abigail too long and too often, and she caught her father and Nabal exchanging glances several times throughout the meal. As soon as the poached apricots had been served, Abigail excused herself and escaped to the upper room.

Anna was waiting for her, directing Talia and Channah, two of her other maids, to prepare Abigail's bed for the night.

Kai and Yelena were helping the cook in the kitchen. Her father had given her these four maidservants besides Anna, her nurse, and they had become more like friends than servants.

Anna helped her slip off her embroidered dress, gathering the fine material and folding it neatly. "Who is the man your father invited to stay?"

"His name is Nabal. He is from the town of Maon. He raises sheep in the area of Carmel. Evidently he has a lot of sheep."

"So he is wealthy." Anna eased her into the looser, cooler dress she wore to sleep.

"I suppose." Abigail was not impressed by wealth. Ira was not wealthy, but he was kind, and that mattered more.

Anna did not respond, but her face showed that there was something she was not saying. "What is it, Anna?"

"I wonder if there is a reason he is here tonight."

"He does business with my father. He was in the area, and he needed a place to stay."

"Yes, that is true," Anna said softly. "But I wonder if there is another purpose to his staying here."

"A purpose? What do you mean?"

Anna made a great show of carefully folding the discarded dress. "You are a beautiful girl, you are of marriageable age...."

As her voice trailed off, Abigail felt a jolt in her chest. "You don't suppose he's here for..."

"To speak to your father, mistress?"

Could Anna be right? But surely her father wouldn't entertain the thought. It was Ira she wanted. Her mind raced. She must let her father know right away that she would only have Ira. She had no brothers or sisters, and her father had always indulged her. Surely he would listen to her.

The morning came quickly, and though Abigail had slept poorly, wrestling with her thoughts, she rose. When her maids had seen her suitably dressed, she hurried down the stairs to speak with her father. She found him in the courtyard speaking with Nabal, who had his traveling cloak and his bag in hand.

Nabal smiled at her, but there seemed no warmth behind the smile. The eyes that gazed at her held something else. "I regret that I have to leave so early, but your father and I have completed our business and I must return to my home. We shall see each other again soon."

With a knowing look at her father, he strode out the gate and was gone.

Abigail turned to her father. "Abba, I must speak with you. There is something I must tell you."

"Ah, my Abigail, first, there is news I have for you that cannot wait." There was a look of resignation on his face.

Abigail held her breath. She did not want to hear what her father was about to say.

"I have chosen a husband for you."

"But Abba—"

"Nabal is a good man, and wealthy. He will take good care of you, and you shall be mistress of a large home. You will be able to take your maids with you."

"But I don't want—"

But once again he cut her off. "It is a fine match." There was a note of finality in his voice. "Nabal shall return for the betrothal, which is set for a week from now."

"But I don't want to marry Nabal." It was improper to argue with her father like this, but then, Abigail had never been known for holding her tongue. Her impetuous nature had gotten her into trouble many times over the years, and none of the reasons she'd acted disrespectfully were as important at this one. "There is someone from the village I want."

A pause, and then, "The rug maker's son cannot provide the kind of life you deserve."

"But I don't need fine things. I don't mind living with less."

"I know you think that now. But in a few years, you will realize the wisdom of my decision."

"But Ira is kind. He is funny. I enjoy talking with him."

"He is unsuitable. With Nabal, you will have your own household, with many servants and many fine things. Nabal is a good man." He turned as if to go and then stopped. "You will prepare yourself for the betrothal in one week's time." He reached out and patted her shoulder, and then he walked out of the courtyard.

She felt tears sting her eyes as she watched him go.

CHAPTER TWO

The week passed far too quickly for Abigail, and word of the betrothal had already passed through the village. She saw Ira in the marketplace, standing a short distance away, but as a nearly betrothed maiden, she could not speak with him. He looked at her, clenching his fists. His eyes said all she wanted to know. Anguish rose up in her heart, knowing what could never be. He gave her a brief nod and then turned and quickly walked away.

She watched his retreating figure, fighting the urge to go after him, but finally she turned away. She would be married soon. She must start acting like a grown woman.

In the marketplace the women gathered around her, chattering about the coming betrothal. She beamed at them and pretended to be happy about her news, yet as soon as possible she excused herself and returned home with Anna.

At the house, she went upstairs and began to pace the floor. "Maybe I should throw myself out the window."

"Mistress, there is no need to spout foolishness. Young women have gone to marriages arranged by their parents for centuries." Anna put her hand on Abigail's arm. It was a familiar gesture the other maids would not attempt, but Anna had been her nurse since she was born.

"Then what can I do, Anna?" Abigail stopped and shook her head. "There is something about him that makes me uneasy. I don't think he is all he seems."

"Mistress, you have always had a good mind. You will make the best of this marriage. Who knows, you might be very happy with him. Love is something that grows in a marriage."

"Not with someone like this. His name means 'fool.' What sort of people give their child such a name? What if he lives up to it?"

Anna hesitated a moment before answering. And then she spoke slowly, as if carefully choosing her words. "Your father loves you. He has chosen the man he believes is best for you."

"But he is wrong." It came out more like a wail than she intended. "Ever since *Imma* died, he is different. He does not care about anything but himself."

Again, another pause as Anna considered her words carefully.

"Your mother's death changed him," Anna agreed. "But the marriage between your parents was arranged. They grew to love each other deeply. The same will happen with you and Nabal."

Abigail considered her words. Her parents' marriage had been arranged, and she remembered the tender looks between them. They had fallen in love after their marriage. Could the same thing happen with Nabal? Abigail didn't see how it was possible.

The week passed quickly, and soon Nabal arrived for the betrothal. She bowed her greeting and appraised him more closely. His beard was full, and there was no gray in it. He was not bad looking, she decided. He wore clothing of the finest linen, and there was a gold chain around his neck with some sort of key on it. There were gold rings on his fingers. He took Abigail's hand and bowed low over it.

"I am the most fortunate of men, my lady."

He and her father had already discussed the bride price at his previous visit, so there was no delay. Because he was not a young man and lived alone, he negotiated himself, and his father was not involved. Their steward, Remiel, and her maidservant, Anna, acted as witnesses as the bride-to-be and the groom-to-be signed the betrothal contract.

After the business had been conducted, Nabal gave a slight bow and presented Abigail with a jeweled box containing a beautiful gold necklace and earrings. Gold jewelry was one of the traditional gifts for the bride, but these were exquisite, the gold intricately worked and of the highest quality. Shyly, she thanked him and went out. She went to speak to the cook about the meal, which, per her father's wishes, would be lamb. She stayed longer than was truly necessary, but she did not want to run into Nabal again.

Finally, when the cook hinted she needed Abigail to leave so she could get to work, Abigail went out to the room where she kept her loom. She sat down and began working the fine woolen thread. She had spun this wool herself, and it was soothing to see it come together, one fiber at a time, into a piece of cloth. Her mother had taught her how to weave, spending long hours hunched over the loom, teaching Abigail how to keep the tension just right and how to work patterns into the fabric with different colored threads.

Abigail had been working for more than an hour when Kai came to summon her. "It is time for dinner, mistress." Kai was the youngest of the maids and had big brown eyes and smooth brown skin.

"Thank you." Abigail rose and started toward the room where her father often sat in the afternoon. As she walked, a movement in one of the rooms caught her eye, and she turned to see Nabal running his hands over one of their carved chests. It had belonged to her grandmother. As she watched, he walked around the room, taking in the thick rugs and the fine furnishings.

Abigail drew back and hurried on. Nabal soon joined them at the table, and when they were seated, Abba raised a cup of wine. "Let us celebrate the joining of my daughter, Abigail, to Nabal of Maon. This day she is betrothed to him as his wife."

A cup of wine was placed in Abigail's hand and then her father and Nabal raised theirs, clearly waiting for her to raise hers.

"I have come to this house for your daughter, Abigail," Nabal said, watching her. "To take her to wife. She is now my wife, and I am her husband from this day forward."

A heaviness settled on Abigail's heart. She fought the urge to run away again. That would forever shame her father. Marriage to Nabal was an opportunity to have her own household, she thought, and in time, a family. She would remain in her father's home for several months, until the wedding ceremony, after which she would move to Nabal's home. They had chosen the month of Sivan, after the wheat harvest. She took a deep breath, gave Nabal a brief smile, and sipped the wine.

The meal was sumptuous. A lamb had been dressed and roasted, and there were her father's favorite capers and mint over squash, leeks with olive oil and vinegar, and loaves of fine leavened bread. She'd added her special fig cakes, dates stuffed with walnuts, and grilled quail. Baskets of fruit and cheese were plentiful.

Nabal did not appear to take too much wine, and Abigail convinced herself that was a good sign. At least her husband would not be a drunkard.

After the meal, Abigail retreated upstairs to get ready for bed. But as she approached the room, she heard Anna's voice.

"It was *how* much?" Anna's voice was muffled, like she was trying to make sure she was not overheard.

"Four hundred shekels!" That was Yelena.

Anna gasped. "I've never heard of that amount for a bride price!" Then, a moment later, she added, "Of course, our mistress is lovely and charming and so intelligent. She is worth far more than that, even. But still. It makes me wonder."

Perhaps she should have been pleased by the praise, but all she felt was the heaviness on her heart increase.

"I did wonder why Ezra was so anxious to sign the betrothal contract," Yelena said.

"It did seem fast," Anna agreed.

"But surely you have noticed changes," Channah said. "There is not as much food as before, and not as fine quality. The linen isn't as fine either."

Abigail had known these things, of course. The sums her father gave her to run the household had shrunk in recent months. But she had assumed he had been cutting back for a short time, in order to make the needed improvements to the clay and straw roof of their home, which had begun to leak during the rainy season. But was it more than that?

"Mistress's new husband is wealthy," Yelena continued. "But I worry that he is not all he seems."

Anna said something, so quietly that Abigail could not hear, and Abigail decided it was time to reveal herself. She made a show of walking toward the room, loudly enough that they could not help but hear her.

"You are back," Anna said, taking a hasty step back from Yelena. "Did you have a nice evening?"

"The food was delicious," Abigail said. When she didn't elaborate, she caught a knowing look between the two servants.

That night she lay in the darkness, listening to an owl calling to its mate. Her father had been so attentive when she was little. She was an only child, and he had doted on her, and, seeing her interest in his papers, had even taught her to read. He delighted in how quickly she understood the letters and figured out how to combine them. He had made her promise not to tell her friends, or it would spread around the village, and then everyone would know—and what man would want to marry a woman who could read? But Abba had been proud of her quick mind and had even joked that if she had been born a boy, she could have been a king.

Yet when her mother died, he seemed to change. He buried himself in his work and spent most of his time around the farm and fields. In recent years, he had also spent far more time sharing strong drink with his friends. Imma's passing had changed them all.

She prayed to Yahweh, asking for a way out, or, failing that, strength and peace over her father's decision. But questions still swirled around in her head. Did Abba need money badly enough that he would sell her to Nabal? Her father loved her. Surely she could have helped in some way. The reality was like a stone in her heart. She turned on her mat and began to weep silently.

The next day, Abba took Nabal around to introduce him to their neighbors and friends. Showing him off, Abigail thought uncharitably. Abba seemed pleased with the respect the association with a man of such means afforded him.

Abigail willed the months to go more slowly, but they seemed to fly. She walked the halls and looked at the items her mother had brought to her own marriage twenty years before. Word had come that there was no need for her to bring any of those things to her home with Nabal, as the house was already furnished.

One morning, in the month of Nissan, she gathered up her courage and approached her father to beg to be released from the marriage contract. She knew such an act would bring shame on her family, but it would be better than being sent to live with Nabal.

"I have indulged you too much," was her father's terse reply. "I have been too lenient, and now you do not know your place."

"I do, Abba, but—"

"You must not speak to your husband the way you speak to me. You will learn to keep quiet, as is expected of a woman."

"I will never learn to keep quiet, not when there are things that need to be said."

Abba let out a long sigh. "I pray that you do learn, or your marriage will be an unhappy one. May Yahweh forgive me for the way I have spoiled you. I fear you will pay for it in the coming years."

Abigail did not know how to answer. She ran the hem of her linen robe through her fingers, trying to find the words to say what she felt.

"Nabal is a good man," her father finally said. "You will be happy with him. You will see. But you must learn to think before you speak or act. You will not be able to get away with the things I have let you get away with."

"I believe there is more to him than there seems."

Abba let out another sigh. "It is a good marriage. But even if I wanted to cancel the marriage contract, I could not." He gestured at the new roof, which had been installed the previous month. "Much of the bride price has already been spent."

That was when Abigail knew for certain that there was no changing what was to come.

Her wedding day arrived as expected, and as she stood at the window of the small second-floor room where she'd slept so many nights, she wondered what the day would hold. Before the sun set, the ceremony would be over, and in a few days' time, she would leave her home forever.

She turned as the maids came to dress her. Talia combed her hair, which cascaded down her back. It would be worn down in public for the last time today.

She stood quietly as Channah and Yelena dropped her wedding tunic, embroidered with golden threads, over her head. Then Kai, the youngest of her maids, carefully placed Abigail's headband of gold coins above her forehead and drew the veil over her face.

Abigail smiled at Kai, remembering when the girl had come to her. Kai was the oldest of eight children. Her parents were poor, and her father had come to the house one day with her in tow. She had looked to be around twelve years old.

"Do you have a place for her, mistress?" he had inquired. "She is a hard worker. She could help in the kitchen."

Abigail had looked at the thin young girl standing in front of her. The child's large brown eyes were pleading, and Abigail understood that the family didn't have enough food to go around.

"I will find a place for her. Thank you for bringing her to us."

The father had nodded, obviously relieved, and pushed Kai forward. "Don't be any trouble to the mistress."

Abigail had spoken to the father. "Go to the kitchen and tell the cook I sent you. She will have something you can take to your family."

"Thank you, my lady." He had turned and, without a backward glance at his daughter, hurried around to the back of the house.

The other maids, knowing their mistress, took Kai in hand, and the cook found work for her to do in the kitchen. In time, Anna taught Kai how to be a maid to Abigail.

Now, Kai placed a crown of leaves atop Abigail's veil. "You are beautiful, mistress," she said shyly.

Suddenly there was the sound of women's voices in the entry of the house. Neighbor women had come from all around to witness the wedding festivities and help in the preparation. Abigail, glancing at them through her veil, put a welcoming smile on her face. They would all see a happy bride.

The women murmured as they milled around the room, taking in the decorations and inquiring about the wedding feast. Their husbands milled around the courtyard, discussing crops and animals and waiting out the time.

Anna told the women what was being served, and they nodded in pleasure. It would be a lavish wedding, and they were glad to have their families here today.

A woman named Eliana patted Abigail's shoulder and murmured, "You will make a beautiful bride, Abigail."

"You are fortunate to have found such a rich man for a bridegroom," added Gilah, a grain merchant's wife.

Abigail wondered how Ira was. She had learned he'd become betrothed and would be married soon himself. She hoped he would be happy.

Malka, one of the girls Abigail knew as a child, approached her. She had been married last year and her belly was round. It would not be much longer before her first child came. Malka beamed and murmured, "Blessed are you, Abigail, for securing such a prosperous husband! May you have many sons!"

"Yes," another woman said, "we hear he is a man of means."

To Abigail's dismay, Zillah and Golda, two women known for gossip, whispered nearby, loudly enough for Abigail to hear them.

"I don't think she's fortunate. Did you see the groom when they were betrothed?"

"Of course. He may be rich, but he was ill-mannered. Didn't have a kind word for anyone except her father. Stingy, he is."

Jael, a woman who was married to one of her father's workers, spoke up with a kinder voice. "Abigail is beautiful, not only of face, but I know her character. She's a woman of great faith."

Zillah sniffed. "It will take faith to be married to that man!"

Abigail could only hope they were wrong. She could find no words to respond to their cruel comments, so she just sat quietly, praying and waiting for Nabal to arrive. As she considered her bridegroom, she fought down the apprehension that rose like bile in her throat. Who was this man who was to become her husband?

Time inched by, and the women, tired of speaking about the bridegroom, occupied themselves with the local gossip and peering out the window for a sign of the bridegroom. They sounded to Abigail like a hive of bees.

The women waited what seemed like most of the day. Toward evening, Nabal, having ridden a long way from Maon to Abigail's home, came at last and knocked loudly. Remiel appeared, heading for the door, but one of the women sprang ahead of him and opened the door. He scowled at her.

All eyes were on the bridegroom. "I have come for my wife," he announced.

Abigail rose and was led to the doorway. Nabal placed her arm on his, uttering the traditional words, "A treasure indeed! Rejoice with me, my friends, for a more beautiful maiden cannot be found!" His eyes traveled the length of her body, and his eyes glittered. Abigail took a deep breath, and her heart pounded.

They walked to the courtyard, where they were greeted by her father and their guests.

"My wife!" Nabal announced. The people cheered and clapped. Abigail and Nabal were led to the place of honor at the table and the wedding feast began.

Abigail forced herself to keep a smile on her face, doing everything that was expected of her. She smiled as gift after gift was presented. There were pillows filled with feathers, embroidered wall hangings, and hand-woven rugs, but none of them made her feel better.

The wedding feast was as lavish as the betrothal feast: goat cheese and olive appetizers with fresh melon, saffron millet with raisins and walnuts, roasted lamb, grilled fish, leavened bread, fig cakes, and honey-almond stuffed dates. Wine flowed freely, and Abigail watched her new husband partake of more than one goblet. Then they were escorted to her own sleeping chamber, which had been decorated with fresh flowers by her maids. With suggestive comments and laughter, the neighbors wished them well. Then she and Nabal entered the room and Nabal closed the door. Her mouth felt dry and she bowed her head, praying silently.

God Who Sees Me, grant me the strength this night to endure what I must.

Nabal pulled her to him, his eyes glittering and his breath heavy with the wine. He tugged at her dress, and the wreath and veil tumbled to the floor, as did her headband of coins. He carried her to the bed and laid her down more roughly than was necessary. Her introduction to the intimacy of marriage was swift and bumbling. There were no loving words, only a deed hastily done by a drunken husband. Someone waited outside the room to receive the bloody cloth. When Nabal swaggered to the door and handed it to over, someone made a lewd remark and Nabal pushed the door closed. He staggered to the bed, a smirk on his face, and passed out.

Waves of pain swept over her as she crept from the bed to wash herself in a basin that had been provided by Anna. She wept silently and vowed then that only the Lord God would see her tears.

Nabal took her again in the morning before they went down for their meal. She'd cried out in pain, and when he left her to dress, struggled to quench the sobs that rose in her throat. Then, after he had dressed, he returned to her and told her that he must return to Maon as soon as possible, so they would be leaving today. Abigail felt the breath leave her lungs. They were supposed to have more time before she had to leave, before she had to say goodbye to her father and her home.

"We cannot leave. Not yet. I have not packed my things."

"Then you had better pack them quickly. We leave after breakfast."

Abigail could see that arguing with him would be useless, so she tried a different tactic. "But—husband." She stepped closer and touched his arm gently. "We have hardly begun to enjoy the marriage week." She had to choke out the words. "Surely you can't mean to—"

"I mean what I say." Nabal pulled his arm away from her. "Your father promised me you were obedient. Don't make me tell him I was misled."

Abigail had no answer. Nabal went out the door, and she stood still, taking in all that had happened. And then she realized she needed to get started packing.

Abigail readied herself and her maids to go, and then she said goodbye to Abba. When he saw her face, he raised his eyebrows and pursed his lips, but Abigail quickly occupied herself with making sure her maids had packed everything. She and her maids would ride in a wagon her father had provided. It had a canopy over the top to protect them from the sun. Nabal rode his horse and was obviously anxious to leave.

Abigail was still feeling tender, and the ride in the wagon did not help. Anna sat next to her and put a comforting hand on her arm. "You will heal, mistress. It is natural for the first time."

She nodded. She would not break down in front of her servants, for they would know what Nabal was like in time. She could confide her anguish with Anna, but only when they were alone. The law said she was to respect her husband, but it would take all her courage.

CHAPTER THREE

Nabal's home was large, and it was fitted with many beautiful things: thick rugs and beds covered with finely woven fabric and furniture made of beautifully carved cedar. But it felt cold and impersonal, as if the furnishing had been chosen more to show off Nabal's wealth and good taste than to showcase his own preferences. Still, Abigail kept the home clean and well run, managing the servants efficiently. There was one room that no one but Nabal was allowed to enter, a room he kept locked with a little key he wore on his neck. Though she was curious, Abigail did not trouble herself with the room. It was one less space for her to worry about.

Abigail was also responsible for the aspects of his business he could not be bothered with, such as making sure his workers were fed during the harvest and shearing. She would pack up the fig cakes, the bread, and the wine, and bring it to him and the workers on the backs of donkeys. This way the work did not have to stop while the workers went home to eat, and he took the cost of the food out of their pay.

Nabal invited many business associates into their home and expected his wife to supervise the staff in preparing lavish meals with many fine ingredients. She appreciated the ability to go to the market and select whatever vegetables and meat and cheeses she wished, for though usually Nabal kept track of his money carefully, he did not spare expenses when there was someone he wanted to impress. They hosted a lavish Passover feast and invited most of the village, because even though Nabal did not care much for prayers or for the rituals of their faith, he loved to show off his wealth.

Abigail had many fine things, but she was lonely. This village was small and high up in the hills. Most of the inhabitants worked for Nabal, in the vineyards or the orchards or with his flocks, which grazed in the fields between here and Carmel. Her husband was a great man in the village, but there were not many women to talk to. The women she met in the market treated her differently because she was the wife of Nabal, and their fortunes rested with him. She missed the easy friendships of her youth. She missed so many things about her old life.

Nabal asked her each month why she was not yet pregnant, and she did not have an answer.

"The Lord will bless us in his time," Abigail said.

"Your God is not worth much if he cannot give me sons," Nabal said with a sneer. Abigail pushed back the tears that threatened to spill over. Yahweh was not just *her* God. He was the one true God, and she knew Nabal had represented himself as a devoted follower to her father in order to win her hand. Abba would not have allowed the marriage otherwise. She would continue to pray. Yahweh would bless them in His time.

So it was with great rejoicing that Abigail found herself with child a year after their wedding. At last she would have someone to love and care for. Nabal took the news as a matter of course. With no apology for the unkind words he had flung at her previously, he acted as if his prowess as a husband could produce no other result.

He wanted a son and made it clear he expected her to give him an heir. She let the words roll off her. Happiness filled her at last. If it was a girl, she could teach her to spin and weave. There were also cooking secrets her mother had passed down to her, and she could teach a daughter those.

She went about her duties with a smile on her face. Eliab, their steward, took some of her tasks upon himself when he was not doing the accounting and acquiescing to the requests of his master. She spent more time weaving, imagining blankets and garments for her little one.

When she felt the first movements of her child, she was filled with wonder. Did all new mothers feel as she did, knowing a living child grew within her?

Her father, hearing the news, sent word that he was pleased at the prospect of a grandson. She shook her head. Why did men always assume it would be a boy?

As the months went by, she had an unexpected respite from Nabal. For once he made sure she had what she needed, and though he was still gruff, he was as kind as his nature allowed. She thanked the Lord God every morning in her prayers for the promise of new life He had given her.

When she was into her seventh month, the winter rains came and the house took on a gloomy tone. Abigail and her maids piled light rugs on their beds, only to shiver with the dampness.

One night there was a loud clap of thunder, and Abigail was awakened. A sharp jab of pain coursed through her back and she wrapped her arms around herself, stifling a cry. She rolled over and tried to go back to sleep. It must be a false labor pain. The midwife had warned her she might have those as her time grew closer. She was still almost two months from when the child would come.

She listened to the wind blowing through the slits in the stonework, but the pains did not subside. Instead, they became harder, more intense, and more regular. She became frightened. This was not the weather for the midwife to come to her.

Abigail tried to stifle a moan, but she could not. Anna rose and came to her.

"It is nothing," Abigail said. "It is false labor."

Anna did not answer but put a cool cloth on Abigail's forehead. She held her hand as the next wave of pain coursed through her, and Abigail did not recognize her own voice in the moaning that filled the room. After the pain had passed, Anna awakened the other maidservants.

"Tend to our mistress," she ordered, "I will send for Bina." Anna sent Kai to find a male servant to weather the storm and bring the midwife. Abigail prayed that she would get there in time.

Yelena wiped Abigail's face with a cloth, and twice she and Talia tried to hold her over the birthing stool.

Bina finally arrived with her bag of herbs. She examined Abigail and shook her head. "When is the baby due?"

"Not for two months," Abigail gasped between jabs of pain.

Bina clicked her tongue. "This child is too early. That is not good. We must deliver it quickly." Bina mixed some herbs in a cup of water. "Drink this. It will help with the pain, my lady."

Abigail did not know what was in the foul mixture that Bina had given her, but it did not stay down long enough to do any good. For that night and part of the next day, Abigail struggled, alternately being lifted over the birthing stool and laid down on her bed to rest for a few moments. She could hear Nabal asking what was wrong and why his son had not yet been born.

"Does he think he can just order the child to be born?" Anna hissed in her ear.

Dawn rose on the second day, when at last the baby slipped into Bina's waiting hands.

"You have a son."

Abigail sighed wearily. At least Nabal would be pleased. She had produced an heir. "Let me see him."

Bina was working over the baby, firmly striking the baby's back.

There was no cry, and his skin had a grayish tinge.

"I am so sorry, my lady. He does not breathe." Bina shook her head. "The cord was wrapped around his neck. It must have choked him in the birthing. He is very small and born too early."

The cry that came out of Abigail's throat sounded almost animal.

Anna took her hand. "I'm sorry, mistress." Her servant could not hide the tears that ran down her cheeks.

"No. It is not true." Abigail reached for the child, and reluctantly, Bina wrapped the baby in a soft cloth and put him in Abigail's arms. She looked down at the perfectly formed face, seeking signs of life, but there were none. His skin was turning blue, and his chest did not rise and fall. She touched the tiny fingers. Tears slipped down her cheeks.

Nabal was sent for, and he burst into the room. "My son is dead?" He stared down at the bundle in Abigail's arms, and to her surprise, his eyes filled with pain. He blinked as if tears were threatening to spill over. Then he suddenly turned and looked accusingly at Bina. "What did you do to him?"

Bina looked him in the eye. "He was dead when I delivered him," she answered. "He was born too early, and also the cord was wrapped around his neck and choked him in the birth canal."

For a moment Abigail thought he might strike Bina for her insolence. Then the anger faded, and his shoulders sank. He looked dazed, as if all life had gone out from his body.

"Bury him," he said suddenly, turning to go. "A dead son is of no use to me." And then he walked out of the room.

Abigail did not want to let go of the child. She held his cool form to her breast, crying and wailing. Finally, though, Anna whispered soothing words while Yelena pried the dead child from her arms, and the baby was prepared for burial and taken from the room. Abigail wept, her heart breaking for her lost child. Alone, she asked forgiveness for the thoughts she harbored against her husband and struggled with her faith as she tried to understand why the Lord God had allowed her to lose her child. Perhaps Nabal had been right. What good was faith in Yahweh when He could not give her the thing her heart most desired?

❖

Little by little, Abigail regained her strength over the ensuing weeks. She forced herself to resume her duties running the household, and she was grateful for the faithful servants, and especially their steward, who had done what was needed to keep the estate running while she recovered.

Her father had sent a message:

Daughter, I grieve with you at the loss of my grandson. Strengthen yourself, for I am sure you will have other children. Your loving father, Ezra of Carmel.

She read the brief message and a longing rose up in her heart to return to her home and seek the comforting arms of her father, as she had done as a child. She sighed. She was a grown woman, not a child. She put the scroll away.

In her dreams she still saw the small, perfect face, the long lashes of the eyes that would never open. She had curled his tiny cold fingers around one of hers and breathed in the scent of him. He was a part of her that would live in her heart all her life. Nabal would not talk about him or give him a name so Abigail quietly named him Akim, which meant *originating from God*.

She did not understand why he had died but believed in her heart that it was the Lord God who gave and took away.

She strengthened her spirit, praying for strength to go on. Perhaps the Lord would grant her another child one day.

She dreaded the time when her husband would once again order her to come to his bed. Though he was forced to wait until she had completed her forty days of purification for a son, Nabal called for her as soon as she was no longer unclean.

But months went by with no sign of another child. Abigail endured Nabal's fumbling, but in her heart she felt the Lord had closed her womb, and her earnest prayers brought no change. Nabal berated and belittled her for her "failure," but she let the cruel words roll off. She had learned to put herself in a private place in her spirit, where he could not touch her soul.

CHAPTER FOUR

❖

Abigail paused in her weaving and listened. The angry voices from the courtyard grew louder. Her husband had cheated one of his workers on his pay again. This time it was Phineas. She sighed. Phineas was a good man and a hard worker. She rose and went to the doorway facing the courtyard. Many times she had taken food and other provisions to Nabal's workers, including the family of Phineas. The angry worker looked up and saw her standing there quietly. He looked back at Nabal and, shaking his head, he suddenly turned on his heel and walked away.

Nabal walked toward Abigail, waving his hand in the direction of Phineas.

"You see, once again I have prevailed. They need to be content with their wages. Always asking for more than they are entitled to."

The injustice angered her, but she remained calm, her voice soothing. "You have not found it necessary to raise their wages, then?" He was oblivious to the edge behind her words.

"If I am not cautious with my money, how would you have the means to run my household?" He tilted her chin with his finger and gave her a knowing smirk.

She had learned to steel herself against recoiling at his touch. In three years of marriage, she had learned deference when it was necessary but also how to rebuff him whenever possible.

She needed to redirect his thoughts. "I have inspected the storehouse, and all is in order. You will be hiring more shearers soon?"

"I will be traveling to Carmel to make sure my lazy shepherds give me an accurate count of the sheep."

She waited. In the first year of their marriage, he had questioned every purchase and inspected every article in the storehouse for fear she would waste his money on unnecessary goods. But having been well taught by her mother and then tutored in Anna's capable hands, Abigail knew how to run a household and handle her servants. Reluctantly, almost begrudgingly, Nabal had finally trusted her to run his household as she wished. Nabal held on to money as though it were a favored child, but he gave what she needed to run the household. To her amazement, he did not ask about her weavings, which she quietly sold in the marketplace. She used part of the money to help the families of their workers.

He touched her arm and murmured, "The day is ending. Perhaps there are other ways to spend our time."

She bowed her head. "My lord, the time of women came upon me this morning."

Nabal scowled. She knew he did not like being thwarted in this particular pursuit, but he had to respect the laws of Moses. He could not lie with her if she was unclean.

"How can I ever have a son if you will not let me near you?" His eyes narrowed. "Perhaps I need a second wife, one more capable of accommodating me." He turned and stalked away toward the barn.

Anguish rose up in her heart. She had borne Nabal a son, and his loss haunted her every day. She felt hollowed out and fought back tears. She watched Nabal for a moment and then turned back to the house. She could not let him unsettle her.

She lifted her chin and walked quickly back into the house. She returned to her loom, sending the shuttle through the threads a little more forcefully than needed.

That evening Abigail heard Nabal ride out of the courtyard, headed for the wine shop, no doubt. There were women there who would accommodate him, for a price.

It was one more thing Abigail had to endure.

◆

Abigail's father came to visit from time to time. She welcomed him warmly, and Nabal was courteous but distant. Abba usually stayed a week, but Nabal would only give him three days of hospitality, as was the custom to a guest, before taking himself off to the town or ignoring him altogether. Nabal spent his time in the mysterious private room that Abigail was never allowed to enter.

She sat with her father in the orchard one afternoon, and Abba took her hand. "You've had a difficult time, haven't you?"

A breeze stirred the air, and it was cool and fragrant under the sycamore trees. It was the middle of flax season, and Nabal was busy overseeing the harvest, so they did not need to worry about him overhearing.

She nodded. "I have learned to have peace."

"I am sorry, child. I did not know."

"I know, Abba." It had taken her years to come to the understanding that her father had not known what he was sending her into. He had known Nabal as a business associate and had seen that he was prosperous and a good match. He had not known how Nabal could be. Though he had been dazzled by the bride price, she believed that things might have been different if he had realized who Nabal truly was. "The hardest time was the child. I hated him for that."

"I have tried to trust that the Lord was right about that, but it is difficult. I was looking forward to a grandson." He gave her a hopeful look. "There is no sign of another?"

Abigail shook her head.

He patted her hand. "Well, in time, perhaps."

She did not respond. She did not know what to say. She prayed daily for a child, and she tried to believe that Yahweh would bless her when He chose, but inside she was starting to doubt that He cared at all.

"Come," she finally said, rising. "Let me show you the rest of our orchard. It produces grapes, apples, pomegranates, apricots and, of course, dates."

"It is beautiful," Abba said, letting her help him to his feet. He had complained that his eyesight was starting to go, but he still saw well enough to take in the lovely trees. "Will you celebrate Passover?" The feast was not long away. She knew it was important to her father to follow the rules of the Torah, and she was glad to be able to give him the answer he hoped for.

"Yes, of course." Truthfully, last year Nabal had wanted to skip the celebration, frustrated by the hassle and the cost of hosting for their workers and their families. But Abigail had simply ignored his protests and continued on as if she hadn't heard, and, as she'd hoped, he had acquiesced—or, at any rate, he had not stopped her from preparing the feast. And he had been quite pleased with the many thanks the guests had given him.

Her father stared at the ground a moment. "Shall I stay for Passover? I have celebrated with neighbors before, but they are gone now."

"The family is gone? What happened?"

"They were older than I am, and both died within a week of each other. They had no children."

"Oh, Abba, I'm so sorry." She put a hand on his arm. "You have been alone a good deal." She glanced at him and arched her eyebrows. "There is not a nice widow that you could find comfort with?"

"I'm not sure I want to marry again."

"Is living alone in that big house better?"

He shook his head. "Don't rush me, Daughter. If the Lord God wants a wife for me at my age, I'm sure He'll provide one."

Looking at his serious face, Abigail suddenly began to laugh. It bubbled up from somewhere inside, from a place that had been locked up for a long time. She could not picture her father taking a bride. At his obvious consternation, she stopped. "I'm sorry, Abba, I should not laugh at you."

This time he patted her hand. "If it makes you laugh, Daughter, then I will gladly bear it. I fear you do not have much reason to laugh in this house."

Abigail did not want to go down this path again, and quickly changed the subject. "How is Remiel? The household runs well?"

He looked away, not meeting her gaze. "As well as can be expected. Not as it was when the household was in your charge. He grows old, as do I."

She looked at her father more closely. His hair was turning white at the temples and his beard was mostly gray. She didn't want to think of her father growing older. He was all she had. If only she could return home and take care of him. Yet women could not instigate divorce. The husband had to give his wife the *get*, or certificate of divorce. While he threatened sometimes, Nabal needed her to run his household and all the other things he expected her to do. And he loved to show her off to his business associates, calling her the most beautiful woman in Israel, as if his status was raised by the sight of her. He would never willingly give her up.

She put those thoughts aside and smiled at her father. "What news have you brought me? Tell me what is going on outside of Maon." She used to hear all that went on in the village when she went to the market or to draw water, but these days she so rarely heard news from the world beyond these walls.

Abba stroked his beard. "Your friend Rinnah has just had her third child. A boy. A great big gangly thing who looks very much like Rinnah's father."

"Jabin must be pleased." Rinnah was the butcher's daughter, and she and Jabin had played among the streets with Abigail. Rinnah had been delighted when her father arranged a marriage to him a few years back.

"He is showing the child off all over the village."

Abigail was pleased for her friend, but news of her friend's joy brought back her own loss. Her father must have realized why she had gone quiet, and said, "Have you heard about Saul's young commander?"

Saul was the king of Israel, and he resided in Gibeah. "The shepherd boy? The one who killed that giant?" Everyone in Israel had heard the story, though secretly Abigail wasn't sure how much of the story to believe. How could a small boy bring down a giant with one single pebble? It was impossible.

"He is no longer a boy. He has grown into a man and has brought great victory to Saul's armies."

"That is good news," Abigail said, with as much enthusiasm as she could. Men were always thinking about fighting or going to war.

"He has married Saul's daughter Michal. It is said she is very lovely."

This was more interesting. "So he is not just Saul's commander, he is married to his daughter."

"Yes. It is said he paid quite a bride price."

Abigail did not want to discuss bride prices with her father, not after what she'd heard about her own.

"It is a smart way for David to get close to the king," Abigail said. "There is much power in aligning oneself with authority."

"What makes you think David is interested in power?" Abba swatted away a fly that was buzzing around nearby.

"All men want power," Abigail said simply.

Her father did not argue. They walked in silence for a few moments, listening to the sounds of the birds in the trees and the buzz of the bees.

"I do not know what kind of a life it must be when married to a man who conquers villages and slaughters the inhabitants," Abba said.

It took a moment for Abigail to realize he was still talking about David. It was true that the commander did not sound like the kind of man who would hold any appeal for Abigail, but she also did not know that her father had any right to be making such judgments. He clearly did not have the best sense about this.

"I am sure Michal has nothing to do with such things." Abigail had heard stories about Michal, who was supposed to be stunning and graceful and very talented with the needle. "I suppose it is not for us to say."

But as they continued on, Abigail couldn't help but wonder about the princess and her husband.

◆

Shearing time came again, and extra men were hired to help with Nabal's large flocks of sheep. Abigail knew her husband would pay them little, but many men needed money these days and so they took the job. This season meant a reprieve for her, as he spent most of his time at the shearing sheds outside Carmel, watching everything the men did and yelling if he thought they were working too slowly.

However, the burden of overseeing the distribution of food to all these workers still fell on Abigail. She and her servants made trip after trip from Maon to Carmel. Mostly she made sure the donkeys were packed well and there were enough servants to serve the workers when they got there, but Nabal expected her to come with the servants to oversee the distribution and the serving of food to make sure no one took more than his share. It was a grueling task, the ride hot and dusty, and at the shearing shed, she found the bleating of the hundreds of distressed sheep agonizing. But still, Abigail did not mind so much. She got to leave the town, and though she passed through largely empty plains, it was nice to have something else to see.

This day, the donkeys had been loaded with the supplies for the journey from Maon to Carmel, and Abigail, along with her servants, set off. Elisheba and Aya chatted behind her, but they did not involve her in their conversation. The donkeys were familiar with the route, along a narrow, rocky path through the hills, and as she walked beside them, she let her mind wander. Her monthly courses had been irregular for many years now, but it had been many weeks since she'd last bled. Could she be with child? She tried to determine if she felt different, if her breasts were tender or her body tired. But she did not feel any more tired than normal.

Yahweh would bring her a child when the time was right, she knew, but she could not help hoping. She thought back to an encounter with a woman and child in the village. Then her thoughts shifted and she started dreaming about the next fabric she would weave. The dye-maker had shown her a beautiful bright blue, and though it was costly, Abigail had envisioned a fine weave, and she hoped she would be able to make a beautiful covering for the bed.

But... What was *that*?

At first, Abigail did not trust her eyes. It was a great group of people, she thought. It had just looked like a shadow on the hillside, but as she got closer, she saw that it was a vast group, walking slowly toward the wilderness on the far side of the hill. She feared that they were warriors marching on Maon to raid and take the city, but they were headed the wrong direction, and in any case she quickly realized that these were not warriors. They were not dressed for battle, and they trudged through the fields at a slow pace. There had to be at least six hundred men, and they were followed by twice that many women and children.

Who were they? Where were they headed? As she got closer, she saw that at the front of the group was a tall, broad-shouldered man. He was their leader, that was clear from the way he stood, the way he walked, and the way the men jostled for position near him. Abigail watched as the group plodded on, turning her head to continue to watch them as she and her caravan rounded the hill that blocked them from view. Abigail had ridden this route so many times, but she rarely saw another person, let alone hundreds of them.

"That is David and his men, miss," Elisheba said. She must have noticed Abigail watching them.

"David?"

"The king's commander," Aya answered.

"Why would the king's commander be here?" Abigail turned her head again, but the group was hidden by the hill. "If that was an army, it was the saddest army I have ever seen."

"Have you not heard? David has angered the king. He has fled the palace."

"What happened?" And how did her servants always know more about what was going on than Abigail did? "How can that be?"

"It is said that the king is jealous of his young commander. He fears David will overthrow him and take his throne. The king gets more nervous the more people grow to like David, and so he threatened to have him killed."

"King Saul would kill his daughter's husband?"

Elisheba shrugged. "David's wife did not flee the palace with him. It is said her father did not let her go."

Abigail thought about this. It did not sound like much of a marriage—but then again, her own marriage had not been what she'd hoped for either.

"Who are the people with him?" Abigail asked.

"Those are his followers," Ava said. "He is said to have many people loyal to him."

"The women sing that Saul has slain his thousands but David his ten thousands," Elisheba said. She raised her eyebrows. "He is said to be quite handsome."

"Some say that he will be the next king of Israel." Aya brushed back a lock of hair that had caught the breeze. "He was chosen by God and anointed by the prophet Samuel."

"If that is the case, it is no wonder King Saul is afraid of him," Abigail said, shaking her head. "But why is he here?"

"He is hiding from the king." Elisheba said it with such certainty that Abigail could not help it. She laughed out loud.

"He is hiding? With that many people?"

"If you are trying to hide"—Aya gestured toward the hills, which were covered with rocky outcroppings and threaded through with caves—"this is not a bad place to disappear."

Abigail supposed she was right. Those hills were largely unpopulated, and the terrain was rough, unfriendly. There were many places to vanish among those stones.

For some reason, she found herself hoping that David and his men would do just that.

◆

Nearly a week later, she was readying the load for that day's ride. While waiting for the signal that all was ready, Abigail took a few moments to walk in the garden. The sun was already warm on her shoulders, and she looked out over the wall at the wilderness.

She heard them before she saw them—a long, low rumbling that made it sound like the very earth was humming. And then the ground began to shake. She craned her neck, and soon they came into view. The soldiers wore armor that glistened in the sun, and each carried a tall spear. They marched in step, thousands of feet striking the earth at precisely the same time. It was chilling.

"Saul's men." The steward, Eliab, stood next to Abigail. "Coming to hunt for that traitor David, no doubt."

"Traitor?" Abigail was surprised by his words.

"What else would you call him?" Eliab nodded his head toward the soldiers and sniffed. "He is supposed to serve the king, and he has taken some of the king's men and run off with them. Hiding, they say, like a coward." Eliab watched the soldiers walk past for a few moments. All those feet stirred up dust that was blowing toward her home. It would mean a lot of cleaning work for her servants. "Saul must think David and his men are nearby for them to have sent that many men."

"What will happen if they do find him?" Abigail feared she already knew the answer.

"It will not take long for Saul's army to show them all what happens to traitors." Eliab sniffed again. "I tell you what, if I knew where he was, I'd point them in the right direction myself."

Abigail did not respond. Saul had been a good king for years, since the prophet Samuel had anointed him. It was hard to imagine how that ragtag bunch she'd seen trudging through the wilderness could be a threat to the Lord's anointed. Surely sending this many men from the royal army was a sign of the king's insecurity.

"King Saul is determined to find him," Eliab continued. "He will not stop until David has been put to death. And he has ordered that anyone who helps David will be put to the sword."

She watched as the army advanced across the rugged landscape. "Surely he could not mean that."

"He certainly does. We just learned from a messenger who came to the town that Saul had the city of priests destroyed because the high priest gave David food."

Abigail felt her stomach turn. She knew how the world worked by now. She knew that conquering a city for riches and power was a game to men. But she could never get used to it. "Women and children too?"

"Of course. Even the animals. You can't let these kinds of people off the hook. If you disobey the king, you have earned his wrath."

What kind of man could slaughter innocent children to make a point? What kind of person would want to serve such a king? Truly their king was mad.

"Evidently only one priest escaped—Abiathar, son of Ahimelech. Rumor has it he fled to David," Eliab continued. "He would be the first one I ran through with my sword if I found them." He nodded toward the army advancing across the desert. "Let us hope they catch the traitors."

She thought about the figure she'd seen at the front of that ragged group and found herself hoping that David and his men would find a way to vanish, to send Saul's army back to the palace empty-handed. But it was treason to say so.

"Yes," Abigail said with as much enthusiasm as she could muster. "Let us hope they catch the traitors."

◆

For the next few days, Abigail tried to focus as she went about her tasks. There was no more talk of David, but Abigail knew she was not the only one who had seen him and his men marching toward the wilderness of the hills. Any one of the servants who had been with her that day might betray David in order to protect their families. If Eliab was right, King Saul would surely consider it treachery not to report what they had seen. Was she putting her household at risk by keeping quiet? But she could not bring herself to say what she had seen.

But a few days later, as Abigail and her servants were riding back toward home, they saw the king's men returning toward Gibeah. The precise lines and strict rhythm of the previous march were gone, and now each man was walking as fast as possible in the hot sun. Where were they going in such a hurry? Had they found David?

Eliab went to the town, and when he returned he had grave news. The Philistines were attacking Israel again, and the king had recalled his army to fight them.

Abigail knew this was terrible news. The Philistines were Israel's sworn enemies. They were almost inhuman, savages who wanted nothing more than to wipe Israel away completely and take all the land God had given them for themselves. If they had attacked one of Israel's cities, she knew it would be bloody and treacherous. She prayed that the king's army would make it back safely and quickly, and that they would stop the invasion in short order, with few casualties.

But, as she thought about their retreat, she could not help being a bit glad that they had not found David.

CHAPTER FIVE

❖

It had seemed to Abigail, weary from the daily trips to Carmel, that the shearing would never end. But it was, at last, the day of the feast, when they would celebrate the end of the arduous task. More than three thousand sheep had come through the pens this year. They would have more wool than ever to bring to the market to be spun, woven, and dyed. It would be a good year, and the men were ready to celebrate. Abigail had brought twice as many servants with her as usual to the shearing sheds, and they were busy, bringing trays, baskets, and wineskins back and forth to the wooden planks they had set up as tables. They spread out the loaves of bread, roasted lamb, goat stew, and cakes of raisins, and the wineskins were hung nearby. If there was one thing her husband wanted, it was plenty of wine.

Nabal did not pay her any attention unless one of the other men glanced her way. When that happened, he made sure to mention that his wife was both beautiful and obedient, bringing him exactly what he had asked for the feast. Inside, she seethed, but she did not show it. But she overheard one of the workers talking to another: "If I had a beautiful wife like that, I would treat her better. The man lives up to his name—*fool*!" She could not help but smile at that.

The wine was flowing freely, and the men were enjoying the feast as Abigail busied herself in the tent they had erected to prepare the food before it was brought out to the tables. The sound of horse hooves caught her attention, but she knew Nabal would not appreciate her shirking her duties. In a few minutes she heard angry voices, although she couldn't make out the words. Suddenly one of Nabal's shepherds appeared at the entrance to the tent. "Please, mistress. David sent messengers from their hideout to give our master his greetings, but he is doing nothing but insulting them. These men were very good to us. They did not mistreat us, and the whole time we were out in the fields near them they never demanded or took one thing from us. They surrounded us the whole time we were herding our sheep near them—all night and all day—and kept us safe. Please, come see what you can do, because disaster is hanging over our master and over all of us, as his household. He is such a wicked man that no one can talk to him."

Fear gripped Abigail's heart, and she felt her skin tingle. The situation must be dire for a servant to speak about his master that way, especially one as unforgiving and cruel as Nabal.

It was true that they had not lost a single sheep this season. Nabal had been quick to boast that it was because of his powerful reputation, though Abigail credited Yahweh with their protection. But were these men now coming to steal the newly shorn wool?

She stepped outside the tent and immediately saw from their torn cloaks and worn sandals that the strangers were not warriors. But their intentions were not clear to her.

One man seemed to be the leader. He was tall, with shoulder-length hair and a beard that had not been trimmed for some time. His voice was shaking with anger. "It is sheep-shearing time. As I said, while your shepherds stayed among us near Carmel, we watched over them. Nothing was ever stolen from your flocks or herds."

"Are you asking me to be grateful that you did not steal from me?" Nabal took another sip from the cup of wine in his hand. Abigail had lost count of how many times it had been refilled.

"It is due to our protection that the thieves have been kept away."

Nabal laughed. "I have never seen a more pitiful bunch of men. You are trying to tell me that *you* are behind our success?"

Abigail could not believe what she heard. Had Nabal not heard of David's reputation as a great warrior? A conqueror who had raided cities and slain all inside in the service of the king?

The men behind the leader had dismounted and stood next to their horses. Abigail did not see any weapons, but she knew better than to assume they did not have any. She grew more uncomfortable by the moment. What did they want?

"We have six hundred men, just beyond those hills. We are saying that we could have easily taken what we wanted. But we did not."

If Nabal recognized the truth behind those words, he did not show it. He swigged another gulp of wine and swished it around in his mouth before he swallowed.

"We are here to ask that you share your bounty with your protector David at this feast time. Our women and children are hungry, and we have nothing to feed them."

"My protector." Nabal took another sip of wine and spit it out on the ground. "You mean the senseless rebel who is on the run from the king? What is he but a deserter who will be soon extinguished?"

"He is the next king of Israel," a man behind the first said. This man was shorter, stockier, younger, and very strong. "He has been chosen."

Nabal laughed at that. "A shepherd? The next king of Israel?" He took another gulp of wine and set his cup down on a nearby table. "It is ridiculous, and so is your demand for help. Should I take my bread and my water and my meat that I've slaughtered for my shearers and give them to a band of outlaws who have come from who knows where?"

"The law—"

"I do not care about your laws. The king has declared that any who help the rebel will be put to death. You see, I could not help you even if I wanted to."

Abigail could not withhold the gasp that came out of her mouth. The Law of Moses insisted that they help strangers in their land. Their own people had once been strangers in Egypt, and Yahweh commanded them to remember this and to share with those in need. In their tradition, a man would entertain even his worst enemy for at least three days, until the "guest" hurried on his way.

But this was not what had shocked her. Could Nabal not see that David—with his reputation as a fierce warrior and his men who were close enough to raid them tonight—was a bigger threat than Saul, whose armies were occupied fighting the Philistines? Did he not understand how to weigh the cost?

Abigail moved closer to her husband. It was impertinent, impetuous, but if she could get close enough to whisper in his ear, she might be able to convince him to change his mind. Surely she could make him see that nothing but trouble would come of sending these men back to the mighty warrior and his hungry followers empty-handed. Hungry men did desperate things.

Nabal looked toward the hills. "Your men are in those hills, you say?"

The men did not answer. It was obvious, from their glances at the tables where the workers had been fed, that they were hungry. The first man watched Nabal carefully. Abigail stepped closer to her husband.

"I will send word to Gibeah," Nabal said. "No doubt King Saul will reward me richly for information on the traitor's whereabouts."

The first man's hand went directly to his waist, where a small knife was no doubt hung, and Abigail realized that there was no more time to whisper to Nabal. Abigail knew she should not do it. It was foolish—it was not her place to speak. But the words came out of her mouth before she knew what was happening.

"We will share our provisions." She spoke loudly, more clearly than she intended. "We have more food than we need, and wine to spare. You may—"

She didn't even see it coming. Her husband's hand smashed into her mouth, silencing her with the shock and pain. She cried out, putting her hands to her mouth. When she took them away, there was blood. Her vision blurred, and she felt shame and anger and pain all flood through her in an instant. Her lip was throbbing. Through the haze, she saw that Nabal's men were wide-eyed, the servants frozen.

"We have nothing to spare," Nabal said simply. "Go back to your leader and tell him that he is not welcome in these parts."

David's men watched a moment longer. The leader looked at Abigail, and she ducked her head. She had known better. It wasn't a woman's place to speak. But still, it had come as a shock. Nabal did not treat her well, but he had never hit her before.

As the moments passed and no one dared to speak, Abigail realized that the burn of shame she felt was tinged with something more akin to anger. Why should her husband be allowed to speak for them all? Why should this man, who did not understand how dangerous the situation was, gamble with all their lives? Was this really what Yahweh had intended?

"You will be hearing from David," the leader finally said. His cloak fanned out as he turned. David's men followed behind him as they marched out of the camp.

No one said anything for a moment. But then Nabal, trying to recover a shred of dignity, picked up his glass, held it aloft, and said, "Let us not allow these interlopers to spoil our feast."

It took a few moments before anyone moved, but slowly, a hum of conversation began to fill the area. Abigail was grateful that those in attendance had stopped looking at her, and she retreated to the space behind the small storage shed for a moment of peace.

"Here, mistress." Aya appeared, holding out a wet cloth. "This will help."

The cloth was cool, and it felt good against her throbbing lip. "Thank you."

It was not long before Nabal's hired men started to return to their homes, and Abigail and the servants began to clean up and pack away the supplies for the trip home. No one looked directly at her, and she knew they were unsure how to react to her bruised face, but she pretended not to notice.

The ride home felt longer than it ever had before. She knew that what had just happened had changed everything. She did not know how she could face Nabal again after what he had done. But more than that, she did not know if she would ever have the chance. How would David—the warrior, whose reputation for vengeance was well known—respond to being rebuffed? Six hundred hungry men, plus women and children, could make any leader act. Her husband's rash, selfish actions had put them all in danger.

Oh God Who Sees, grant me wisdom as to what to do. Somehow I must redeem us in David's eyes and save us from harm. What can I do?

The donkey's sure feet found purchase on the sunbaked clay, rocking her back and forth. And as they neared Maon, Abigail had an idea. She turned it around in her mind, thinking through all the possibilities, and decided she could not fail to act. Her husband did not understand what was needed, but it was their only hope. She would act as soon as night fell.

CHAPTER SIX

❖

The servants began unpacking the remnants of the feast when they reached home. Abigail nodded, as if she approved, but then she pulled Elisheba aside.

"Gather two hundred loaves of bread, all you can find. Bring two of the largest wineskins hanging in the cellar. Bring five of the sheep that have been dressed for roasting and a bushel of roasted grain. Also, gather one hundred clusters of raisins and two hundred fig cakes. Then repack the donkeys as soon as possible."

Elisheba's eyes were wide, but she nodded and turned, scurrying to fulfill Abigail's request.

Abigail turned to the servants who handled the animals. "Let them have straw and water. They must rest as long as they can so they can make the journey."

The servants scattered, each to their tasks. She did not know if they understood why she was asking them, but they hurried to obey.

Abigail went into the house and with the help of her maid-servants, refreshed herself and changed her clothes for the journey into the wilderness. She must find David before there was trouble. Nabal would not be home this night. He would stay in Carmel, too tipsy with wine to risk the journey home. She did not ask where he stayed when he was in the town.

When at last the donkeys were once again packed, dusk was beginning to fall. She told her servants, "We must hurry. We will find David's stronghold and perhaps, since he wanted food, I will be able to talk to him."

Her heart was beating rapidly, pounding in her chest. It was dangerous to travel at night. There was no telling who they might meet on the road, and most who were out at night would not simply let their group, loaded down with supplies, pass unmolested. And they did not know where David and his men were hiding. The wilderness was vast, the hills studded with caves and outcroppings and many places to hide.

Logic told her that there was no chance they would find David's hiding spot. There was no way they could get to them in time. But Abigail was not relying on logic. She was relying on the protection of Yahweh, the Lord of Israel. Finding David's men and stopping them was their only hope. Her whole household depended on it. She urged her donkey on.

As they rode, she prayed. *Lord God, help me to be successful. I must make up for Nabal's insult to David and his men, for I do not know what he will do.*

A lone hawk circled above them. In the silence of the wilderness, Abigail's servants pushed the animals as much as possible, but the sky was dark as they neared the hills. Patchy clouds blotted out some of the moon's light, so Asaph, one of the servants, carried a small lamp to light the path ahead of them.

"What is that?"

Abigail wasn't sure which one of her companions had spoken, but it was not hard to see what he was pointing toward. From the path that wound toward the wilderness, the only road through the hills, she saw a light. A torch, the flames jumping and spinning. Abigail felt fear grip her body as more dots of fire appeared in the darkness. Five, and then ten, and then so many she quickly lost count. How many were coming toward them? Who were they? What did they want? Were these David and his men, or was this another group? Bandits had been seen in these hills recently, she knew, but this could also be a group of Amalekites or Geshurites or any number of dangerous tribes.

"What should we do?" Elisheba asked.

Inside Abigail was trembling, but she tried to keep her composure. She could not show fear or they would all be lost. The approaching group would have seen the light from the lantern. There was no sense pretending they did not know Abigail's little caravan was here.

"We push on and keep searching for David and his men," Abigail said with as much authority as she could muster. No one had the courage to argue. She might be leading her household into a dangerous situation, but it would be equally dangerous to sit back at home and wait for David and his men to come for them.

As the lighted torches moved closer and cast a glow over the men in the front of the pack, Abigail came to understand how vast the army that approached them truly was. There were hundreds of men, most carrying shields and swords, many riding on horses. These were warriors, marching toward battle.

When the approaching army was close, Abigail gave the signal for her donkey to stop, and the others stopped behind her. The army kept coming toward her, and as the shadows separated into shapes, she saw that one man was in the front of the group. He was tall, with broad shoulders and dark hair. This was the man she had seen leading the group toward the wilderness just a few weeks ago.

This was David, then.

He dismounted from his horse and stood in front of her on the path, watching her. There was something cocky in the way he stood, the wide stance of his feet and the sharp upward jut of his chin. But there was also something that kept her from looking away.

"Who are you?" His voice was deep, both loud and confident.

Abigail slipped from her donkey and fell on her knees before David, her face to the ground. "I am Abigail, my lord. My husband Nabal has done you a very great wrong. I am here to try to right it."

"Stand up."

At first she thought she had not heard correctly, but when she looked up, she saw that David was looking at her, waiting for her to rise. The sword at his waist clanged against his feet as he moved.

"I want to see your face."

Slowly, she pushed herself up to her knees and then she rose to her feet. "Now. Tell me," he said. "Why have you come out here into the wilderness in the dark of night?"

"I have brought the supplies your messengers requested, master. My husband was not willing to share, but I have brought the food you asked for and more. Please. Do not have our blood on your conscience when you become king."

David let his gaze move away from Abigail's face and over to the donkeys loaded down with bags of food and skins of wine.

"Your husband does not know you have come." It was a statement, not a question.

"No, my lord." Abigail kept her eyes averted, both out of fear and because she did not trust herself to be able to look away if she saw him again. There was something irresistible in his gaze. "Please accept this gift that I have brought to my master, and give it to your young men and the people of your camp who follow you so faithfully."

It wasn't his looks that drew her, though he was quite handsome. It was something more about the way he carried himself, as if he had never doubted his decisions or his worth. Like he knew God was behind him, no matter what he did.

"It is dangerous for a woman to travel at night."

"It is dangerous for anyone to travel at night."

He nodded, as if acknowledging the truth of her words. "It is not typical for a Hebrew wife to disobey her husband's orders."

"It is not typical for a husband to sentence his household to death by withholding supplies from the Lord's anointed." She did not realize that she'd believed it until the words came out of her mouth. Elisheba had said David claimed that he had been chosen to be the next king, but it wasn't until Abigail saw him that she'd understood. This man, this warrior, was strong, and that drew other men to him. He was a leader if there ever was one. This was the sort of man God would choose.

"You speak more freely than most women."

"I suppose I do not have much to lose at this point."

"You are brave." He took a step closer to her. "What made you believe your husband has sentenced you all to death?"

"Am I wrong, my lord? You come toward Maon at night, with your swords and shields. You do not…" She did not know how to say this, and she let her voice trail off. He stayed silent, letting her speak. It was disconcerting. What man had ever waited for her to speak, listening to what she said?

She thought about the men he had slain to get the bride price to marry Michal. She thought of the battles he had won for the king. She thought about what Aya had said, that Saul had slain thousands, but David tens of thousands.

"You are not known for your mercy," she finally said.

And then he did something Abigail did not expect. David threw back his head and laughed. The men around him chuckled too.

"No, I suppose I'm not," David said. He did not have a smile on his face, exactly, but there was…there was a look in his eye that she could not identify. She stepped forward and was drawn into his warm brown eyes. His beard was trimmed and his dark hair curled to his shoulders. She had heard of

David the shepherd boy who killed the giant, but this was David the man, the warrior.

"What happened?" He touched his cheek, and her hand reflexively went to her own bruised cheek.

"It is nothing, my lord."

"My men tell me your husband hit you when you tried to speak for them." He reached out and brushed the lock of her hair back and looked at her intently.

Abigail felt her cheeks flame, but she did not answer. She searched his face, which had softened from fierce anger to intense interest in her words. She tried to ignore the pounding of her heart.

"Your husband is a fool." David took a small step back, still gazing at her.

She nodded but did not answer.

"He is a fool. But you, Abigail, are braver than most men." He turned toward his men and gestured toward the donkeys. "This brave woman has offered us these supplies. Go ahead and untie them."

The men did not hesitate. It only took a few moments for the food to be slung over their shoulders.

Then he turned back to Abigail. "You are courageous as well as beautiful. Thanks be to the Lord, the God of Israel, who has surely sent you to meet me. Your actions tonight have saved your household."

"Thank you, my lord." She hadn't realized how afraid she had been until the words came out. She was safe. They were all safe. She had to force herself upright to keep from sagging to the ground with relief. David, obviously seeing her distress, put out an arm to support her. He was strong, and even through her dress her skin tingled where he touched her.

He held her arm for a moment. It was forbidden for a man who was not her husband to touch her, but still she did not want him to let go.

"I am all right." She took a small step back. "I do not need you to support me any longer." What she did not say was that having him so close was making her even more light-headed. She pulled herself away.

"Surely God was looking out for both of us tonight." He held her gaze a moment longer, and then he turned back toward his men. "Joab, Asahel, escort Abigail and her servants back home. Make sure they are not disturbed on the journey."

Two men carrying torches stepped forward. She recognized them as the men who had come to the feast earlier. David walked with her and helped her up onto her donkey. When she was seated, David called out, and the men moved to each side of the path, making a clear space for David to walk through the middle of them. Before he started walking, though, he turned back and said, "Good night, Abigail."

She was aware of his eyes still on her as she turned her donkey toward her home. Her servants followed in silence. No one dared to speak until they were outside the tall wooden door of their home. She thanked the men for their help, and then she and her servants went inside.

The sky was already starting to lighten on the horizon by the time Eliab had let them inside and Anna and Kai helped

Abigail into bed. Though her body was exhausted, her mind would not stop spinning. She thought through the long journey and the encounter with the fearsome warrior David. He had been on his way here to slaughter her and her household for a slight inflicted on him by Nabal. It seemed out of proportion for the offense that was done to him, but he was not a man afraid to act, that was clear. She had been terrified, but her actions had stopped the bloodshed. Surely the Lord had protected her. She praised Him for saving her life and the lives of her servants. They did not deserve to die over their master's selfishness.

She was frightened, humbled, thankful. But also, underneath it all, she was confused. David had been on his way to slaughter her and her household, and yet in his gaze she'd seen nothing but kindness. She knew he thought nothing of raiding a city, taking what he wanted, and killing everyone inside, and yet he had been placated with a few loaves of bread and some lambs. She knew he was an upstart, a rebel, a threat to the kingdom. But she had been inexplicably drawn to him.

Oh God Who Sees, forgive me for my foolish thoughts. You watch over me, and I am grateful.

The household slept late that morning, and they all moved slowly as they went about their tasks. The shearing was over, so she did not have to go to Carmel. Instead, for the next two days, she worked on embroidery and spent time at her loom, listening for the sound of Nabal's return. She promised herself she would not lose her temper when she told him what terror his thoughtless actions had almost unleashed. She prayed that

God would guide her words, that He would use the experience to teach Nabal humility and generosity. She prayed that the Lord would have mercy on them all.

The staff treated her differently after that night. While her maids had always been attentive, now they all hurried to do her bidding.

When Nabal did return on the third day, he wasn't alone. A dozen or more men followed him into the courtyard of the house, and Nabal's only words were to order a lavish banquet be set up in the hall and to let the wine flow freely. Abigail oversaw the preparation of the meal and then retired to her rooms. She knew Nabal would be far from rational for many hours.

Finally, in the wee hours of the morning she heard the guests leaving, and she rose to hurry toward the door. Eliab had also heard them and joined her. Nabal was very drunk, hardly able to stand.

At her instructions, his men carried him to his bed and he fell on it in a dead stupor. They quickly left. Eliab took off Nabal's tunic, which was soiled, and his shoes, and covered him with a light blanket. He sighed and nodded to her as he and the men left. Abigail stood looking down at her husband. A part of her felt pity for him, but that spark of compassion was overridden by the abhorrence for the man who lay in front of her. Scene after scene from the past few years rose up in her heart, and she turned away.

Knowing he would not awaken for some hours, she returned to the room nearby that she occupied. Anna had heard the commotion and was waiting to help her back into bed. "Rest, mistress. You have a great deal on your mind."

"Thank you, Anna." Abigail had told Anna about her meeting with David, and after she recovered from the shock of what could have happened, Anna had put her arms around her. "You are a brave woman, mistress," she had said. "But the master will not appreciate what you have done."

Perhaps he would not, but he must know how his thoughtless actions put them all in danger.

Now, she could hear Nabal snoring heavily in the next room and she closed her eyes, hoping to get some rest for the day ahead. She would need all her wits about her.

CHAPTER SEVEN

Someone was shaking her gently. Abigail opened her eyes. Anna's face was above her. "The master is awake."

The early light of morning was streaming through the window, heralding a day of sunshine, but there was no warmth in Abigail's heart as she nodded to Anna and allowed her maidservants to help her dress. She gathered herself for the confrontation ahead. Squaring her shoulders, she entered Nabal's room. He was dressing carelessly, his fingers fumbling with the sash.

"Where is Eliab when I need him?"

Abigail knew from past experience that his head ached from the amount of wine he'd consumed the night before.

"The shearing is finished?" She knew the answer to the question, but she was stalling, choosing her words carefully. If he noticed the yellowing bruise on her cheek, he did not mention it.

"It is done. You will need to arrange to gather and bring back the supplies left over at the shearing pens."

She sighed. Could he not have ordered the men there to bring the supplies? Now the servants would have to travel to Carmel and back again to bring them. Nabal did not think to save them the trip.

She plunged ahead before she lost her nerve. "You had visitors before I left, asking for hospitality."

"And you spoke out of turn to answer them." He yanked on his sash.

"Our customs dictate—"

"Do our customs also dictate plotting to usurp the king? Because that is what David and his men are doing, make no mistake about that."

She remained calm, keeping her voice even. "Have we not heard, my lord, that the prophet Samuel anointed David as the next king?"

"The God of Israel is not interested in cowards like that shepherd boy, hiding away in the hills, expecting others to take care of him."

Abigail had to fight to keep from arguing back that David was anything but weak. That he was strong, and powerful, and there was something about him that made her think God had indeed chosen him. That Yahweh surely did care about the smallest shepherd boy, as well as the grandest king.

"They are nothing but ruffians," Nabal continued. "Beggars. Some people will take whatever they can and then take some more." He finally managed to thread the sash through the loop of his tunic. "They expect others to take care of them. Why do they not work and earn an honest living?"

Abigail suspected it would be hard to find work when the king was pursuing you, calling for your death, but she said nothing.

"They were lucky I did not send word to King Saul about their whereabouts." He began winding his sash around his ample girth.

"They say he has slain tens of thousands. Did you not fear how he might respond to your rebuff?"

"What was he going to do? He has a few dozen starving men. He could not hurt me."

"He could, and he would have if I had not intervened."

"What are you talking about?" He gathered the sash and tied it off. "You tried to intervene, and you saw what happens to women who don't know their place."

She squared her shoulders and looked him in the eye. "Four days ago I saved your life and the lives of all those in our household."

He stopped and looked at her. "What are you talking about, woman?"

"I'm talking about how I took two hundred loaves of bread and five lambs and two skins of wine—"

"You did what?" He straightened up and started toward her. "After I told you not to—"

"I took the food and the provisions, and I carried it into the wilderness myself."

"It was not yours to give!" Nabal grabbed her upper arm and yanked her closer. His cheeks were turning pink, and he was mad—livid—but Abigail was not going to let him speak over her. Not now. Not ever again. She had saved his life, and he would understand what she had done for him and begin to treat her with respect.

"I took the food into the wilderness myself, and I met David and his six hundred men, swords girded for battle, riding hard toward Maon. He was on his way to slaughter us all."

"He was not."

"He was. David is a warrior. He is capable of killing everyone here and just taking what they need, and that was exactly what he and his army intended to do."

For a second, Nabal seemed to not know how to respond. And then he laughed.

"For a moment, you almost had me worried. That is a good one." He shook his head. "You, nothing but a woman, stopping the king's own commander?" He laughed again.

Abigail had been prepared for him to be angry or afraid or shocked. What she hadn't imagined was not being believed.

"Ask Eliab. Ask any of the servants. Elisheba and Aya came with me, as did Asaph. They watched me face down the army on its way to slaughter us all."

Nabal turned and gestured toward Eliab, who was watching quietly from the corner. "Are you hearing this? Do you hear what she says?"

Eliab didn't answer. He looked just to the side of Nabal and moved his feet quietly.

"Well?" A drop of spittle flew in Eliab's direction as Nabal spoke. "Answer me!"

"I did not go on the journey, my lord. But that is the story I have heard from Asaph."

Nabal paled and was quiet for a moment. Then he said, "You lie."

"They were on their way to pay retribution for your rudeness," Abigail said.

"They were coming here to…" He reached out to rest against the wall. "And you stopped them? How?"

"I fell on my face and begged David to accept my offering of food and asked him to avoid having our blood on his conscience when he became king."

She could see that he was beginning to see the truth of her words.

"They were on their way to kill everyone on our property and take what they needed?"

"Six hundred hungry men will do a lot to feed their wives and children."

"They would have killed *me*?"

"You, and our entire household."

Nabal sat down on the bed. She had finally gotten through to him, she saw. But she did not know what would happen next. Then she saw that his breathing was becoming ragged and sweat began to appear on his skin. Good. He was understanding the full import of his actions, then.

"Leavve mmmee…"

It took Abigail a moment to make out what he had said, as his speech was slurred. She saw that he was holding his head. She knew she should not feel triumph. It was not kind. But she couldn't help but feel just a bit glad that he was so affected by what had nearly happened. Abigail turned and walked away, and Eliab rushed toward the bed. He was helping Nabal recline when she walked out of the room.

Many hours later, Nabal had missed his midday meal and had not risen from bed. Both of these things were unusual, but Abigail did not suspect anything was amiss until Aya came and called her.

"The master is ill, my lady. Shall we call a doctor?"

There was a doctor in Carmel, but his fee was quite high. Nabal did not like to send for him unless it was absolutely necessary. There was a healer here in town, known for her herbs and poultices, but Nabal did not have confidence in her abilities, as he had told Abigail on many occasions.

"What does my husband say?"

"He does not speak."

This was odd. Nabal always had an opinion, especially when it came to spending his money. Abigail pushed open the door and found her husband stretched out on his bed. He was lying still, breathing heavily. He could not speak, and the black part of his eyes had grown so large there was almost no brown left. The right side of his face was twisted into an ugly scowl. Eliab was fanning him.

"Yes, Aya. Send for the doctor."

Nabal's condition did not change in the long hours before the physician arrived, his long robes caked with dust. He had been roused from his evening meal, Aya explained quietly to Abigail, and was expecting a further payment for the inconvenience. Abigail nodded. She did not think Nabal would be arguing about the cost at this point. The doctor looked over Nabal, checking his eyes and feeling his heartbeat.

"Can he speak?"

"He has not spoken in many hours," Eliab said.

"Did he complain of tingling in his arms or legs?" the physician asked.

"I do not—" Abigail started.

"Yes," Eliab said. "He could not feel his hands."

The physician nodded. "I have seen this before. I am afraid there is not much we can do."

"Will he recover?"

"Unless the Lord intervenes, he could remain like this," the doctor said quietly.

"For how long?" However foolish Nabal was, he did manage their property and oversee the fields and livestock. Would this now be added to her other duties she'd had to take over? How would the shepherds and other hired help react to orders from a woman with Nabal as he was? How would she care for him in addition to everything else?

"It is impossible to say," the doctor said.

When the physician had gone, Abigail called the servants and Eliab and told them what he had said, though she was sure the word had already spread through the household.

"I will rely on each of you to do the tasks assigned to you. I am sending word to my husband's family of his condition."

Each one pledged to be of help, and she was grateful for the good rapport she had built with them. The hired men were another matter. She could only hope Nabal had paid the shearers when the job was done.

After they'd gone, she thought about how to send word to Nabal's family. He had made it clear years ago that he wanted nothing to do with them. Early in their marriage, she had asked about them, but he would not speak of them, and he would not tell her why. He had not written to them in years, but in a weak moment, fortified with wine, Nabal had mentioned a brother. Was this brother still alive? She did not know. And she did not know where he lived, in any case, or even his name. But she knew that Nabal had come from a town called Kerioth. She would direct her letter there and pray that it found his brother. She wrote a message and sent a trusted servant by horseback to Kerioth to deliver it.

"Ride as fast as you can," she instructed. It would take him at least two days of riding, maybe three, and then he would need to find the man, if he was even in Kerioth. She watched him until he was lost in the distance and turned back to the house. Even if Nabal's brother was found, Abigail thought, after all these years, would he come?

She'd caught quick glances into the locked room where Nabal worked when he went in or out, and she knew it had a large table and important papers, but she had been forbidden to enter from the time she came to Nabal's household. She didn't think their steward was even allowed to go in there. She suspected that was where Nabal kept his money. She thought a moment. There was no other option. She would need funds to handle the household expenses and pay their field workers.

She took a deep breath, approaching Nabal, who lay deathly still. She lifted his head and waited. He did not respond. She carefully removed the key chain from around his neck. She lowered his head and waited a moment to see if he would open his eyes, but he remained still. She turned and swiftly went down the hall to the door of Nabal's private room. As she approached the door, she looked around. All was quiet. Thankfully their steward and the other servants were occupied elsewhere.

She unlocked the door and pushed it open. A strange sweet odor hit her, but she didn't know what it was. It was not stale wine or perspiration. What, then? She moved slowly around the room, lifting papers off the table. She saw a wooden box and opened the lid to find that it contained small leather bags. She opened one. They were filled with a white powder. She sniffed it, puzzled.

"The master used the white powder, my lady."

Eliab stood in the doorway. She jumped, nearly dropping the small bag on the floor.

"You startled me."

He inclined his head. "My apologies, my lady, but I knew sooner or later you would come here."

"You have been in this room, Eliab?"

"I had to tend the master many times when he had used the powder."

She held out the leather pouch. "What is this?"

"It is the white powder that makes men lose their senses."

Opium. She had heard of it but never known anyone who used it. She had thought it was only used by those who lived in the shadowy parts of the town.

"How long has Nabal been using opium?"

Eliab moved closer and looked about. "Many years." A pause, and then he continued. "Something happened in his life, I believe, that he wanted to forget."

She wondered, once again, what had happened between Nabal and his family. What had driven him to this powder?

She shook her head. She could think about that later. For now, she needed Eliab's help. She would be straightforward. "I will need household funds. There is no way to know how long my husband will remain as he is. Do you know where Nabal keeps his money?"

For a moment, it seemed that Eliab didn't know what to say, and seemed to wrestle within himself. He was loyal to Nabal, she knew. Would he refuse her request even now? But then he seemed to come to a decision. "You have been good to us. I will help you, and if the master regains his former self, I will say nothing."

"Thank you, Eliab." She watched with relief as he went to a shelf and moved some scrolls. He lifted out another chest, much heavier, that had been tucked back in some sort of a recess behind the shelf, and placed it on the table. Abigail slowly lifted the lid and gasped. It held a small fortune in gold coins.

She quickly calculated the amount of money she would need to run the household for the next few weeks. She reached in, counted out the sum, and then indicated he could put the box back. "Thank you, Eliab."

"You have had much to contend with, my lady, and each of the servants has experienced your kindness at one time or another. We will do whatever you need."

She could only nod her head. They left the room, and she carefully locked the door. As an afterthought, she turned to

Eliab. "Do you have a key for this room, just in case this one is lost?"

She sensed he knew what she was really asking.

"No. The master wished to keep the only key in his possession."

She nodded and returned to Nabal's room. His eyes were still closed, and he had not moved. She lifted his head again and carefully put the keychain back around his neck. If Nabal awakened, it would be the first thing he would check.

CHAPTER EIGHT

Five days passed, and Nabal remained asleep. The right side of his face was still twisted, and his breathing was slow and shallow. She checked the supplies and sent Eliab to purchase more provisions in the marketplace. She needed to be nearby should Nabal awaken.

Word had spread of Nabal's condition, and merchants who had dealt with her husband came to settle accounts. Thanks to Eliab and access to the locked room, she was able to pay them, and in many cases, gave them more than they expected to receive. She knew the amounts were fair, and they thanked her for her honesty.

Abigail was busy keeping the household running, but she still had plenty of time to reflect on her husband's condition. Had the news of David's actions truly caused him to fall into this state? How could that be possible? And yet the timing seemed irrefutable. After hearing how close he had come to death, Nabal had taken ill, and now he hovered between life and death. It might have been laughable if it was not so horrible. Was this Yahweh's idea of a joke? She did not know. All she knew was that, with each passing day, the man she knew retreated a little further, leaving just a shell of a person on the bed.

On the sixth day, she received word that the extra men hired for the shearing had not been paid and were demanding their promised wages. Abigail had spent enough time looking over Nabal's accounts to no longer be surprised. She sent a message back that she would deliver the payment to Carmel the next day.

"We must make one more trip to the shearing shed," Abigail told Asaph. "Ready the donkeys for the journey at daybreak."

"Forgive me, mistress, but why should you not simply send one of the servants with the payment?" Asaph asked.

Abigail had thought about that, but she knew she could not.

"It is dangerous to travel with that much gold," Abigail said.

"All the more reason to send one of us in your stead."

Abigail shook her head. "When Nabal wakes, he will be furious if he discovers I let that much money out of my sight."

Asaph tried and failed to stifle a laugh, and then, realizing his mistake, he said, "I will make sure the donkeys are ready to go in the morning."

Abigail rose early the next morning and checked on Nabal, but there was no change. He was still lifeless, his face twisted grotesquely, and he grew thinner. She had begun to doubt that he would recover, and she had no idea what that meant for her and her household.

When the donkeys were loaded and ready to go, she slipped the key from around Nabal's neck and used it to unlock his special room. She counted out the gold she would need to pay the men, and then she tucked the box away. Even with the expense of the doctor and all the accounts she had settled in recent days, she had hardly made a dent in the pile. She tucked the gold into a leather pouch, which she tied to her sash, and she locked the door again and returned the key.

The sun shone brightly, bathing the valley in a golden hue as she and Asaph and Elisheba and Aya made their way back along the path to Carmel, hopefully for the last time in a while. There was a breeze today, a blessing, and the rhythmic rocking of the donkey beneath her lulled her into a state of calm. She did not know what would happen with Nabal, but Yahweh did. She did not know if she would ever have a child, but Yahweh did.

As they passed the spot where she had encountered David and his army, she could not help but reflect on that night. It was still chilling to think how close they'd all come to death. She had been lucky....

No, luck had had nothing to do with it, she realized. Yahweh had been gracious, and David had been kind. She had not expected that from the celebrated warrior. He had been kind, and, well, there was something about him that had called her to want to know more about him. It was ridiculous, of course. He had been on his way to slaughter her and her family. There was nothing about that that should make her want to get to know him. And yet there was something about him that intrigued her.

It was not far beyond that spot that she first heard it. Initially, she thought she must be hearing things, the dry, dusty desert conjuring sounds in her mind. But as the breeze blew past her, she heard it more distinctly. It almost sounded like...music.

"Did you hear that?" Aya asked from behind her.

"Yes. But what is it?" Abigail pulled the reins, stopping her donkey, and she climbed off.

"It sounds like a lyre," Asaph said.

Abigail nodded. Was the heat of the desert playing tricks on all of them? She had heard of men seeing visions in the heat of the desert. But she had never heard of music being part of their hallucinations. It was strangely beautiful. Haunting, almost.

"I will go see." Abigail slipped off her donkey. They were still some distance from Carmel, and the earth was dry and dusty, surrounded by hills.

"Mistress. You cannot go alone." Asaph was also slipping off his donkey. "I will come with you."

"No, please, stay here." She knew Asaph had a small knife tucked beneath his cloak. It was more important for him to stay with the donkeys and the bag of gold that she had tied to her animal. "Keep watch over our things. I will go see what it is."

It could be a trick. A ploy to entice travelers off the road to rob them. But she had left her valuable cargo with the servants. There were other things that could happen to a woman, she realized. But for some reason, she did not fear. She could not imagine whoever was making the sweet melody that was carried on the breeze having bad intentions.

The music grew louder as she walked through the brush and around huge rocks, and as she crested the hill, she saw the source. A man, nestled in the shade of a cypress, stroking the strings of the lyre.

He saw her just after she saw him, and he waited a moment and then raised a hand in greeting. He did not seem dangerous. He almost seemed familiar somehow.

She took a step toward him, and he watched her as she walked down the slope. As she came closer, she recognized who he was.

"My lord." She stopped a safe distance from him. A small brook ran past the tree, softly burbling, feeding the grassy growth on which he reclined.

"Abigail." A smile spread across David's even features. "The bravest woman in Maon."

She knew she should be frightened of him. Her servants could not see her on this side of the hill, and she was not sure she could run back to the path before this man could overtake her. This was the man who had slain tens of thousands and who had nearly killed her. But for some reason, she was not afraid. It was not simply that he was wearing a cloak and tunic instead of being dressed for battle. It was more that there was a sense of peace about him.

"Even someone as brave as you should not be wandering these hills alone," David continued. "You never know what sort of ruffians you might encounter."

It was the same word Nabal had used to describe David and his men, but somehow it lost its edge when David said it with that knowing grin on his face.

"I heard the sound of music," Abigail explained. "I thought it odd and came to investigate."

"You thought my music was odd?"

She could not read the look on his face. Was he making a joke? "Not the music itself, my lord. That was beautiful. But it is not a place one expects to hear the strings of a lyre."

"I suppose you are right about that." And then he said, "Abigail?"

"Yes?"

"I am tired of shouting at you. Please step closer."

There were a hundred reasons she should not. It was not proper, her, a married woman, him…well, who he was. He was dangerous. It was not just her reputation that would be ruined if anyone saw her talking to this man alone. It could be reported to King Saul, and the threat would not compare to the danger of the ragtag army she had encountered a few nights before. But still, she stepped closer.

"I will not hurt you," he said, and something in her believed him.

Abigail walked closer and stopped just short of the shade of the cypress tree. "Why are you playing the lyre in the middle of the wilderness?" she asked.

"I wanted to go where no one would disturb me." He looked up at her and grinned. "It seems I chose poorly."

"I am sorry." She started to take a step back, but he held up a hand.

"Please. Don't go." He looked at her, and she saw something in his eyes that made her think he was feeling the same pull toward her that she was feeling toward him. He set the instrument aside.

"I am glad to see you. I have thought about you many times since we met a few nights ago."

She did not want to admit that she had thought about him as well, so she simply nodded. Whatever fear she had felt had disappeared.

"I spent most of my youth in solitude, minding the sheep along the hills outside of Bethlehem."

Abigail nodded. She had heard that he had been a shepherd.

"It is where I first started to write songs to Yahweh. Even now, alone in the wilderness is where I feel closest to our Lord. I like to get away from our camp whenever I can and spend some time writing and praying."

"Is that what you were doing when I heard your lyre? Writing a song for Yahweh?"

"It is." He nodded, and a lock of his hair fell into his face. He brushed it back absentmindedly. "Would you like to hear it?"

She nodded.

David picked up his lyre again, and he plucked the strings.

The Lord is my rock, my fortress and my deliverer.
My God is my rock, in whom I take refuge.
He is my shield and the horn of my salvation, my stronghold.

His voice was clear and melodic, and the music was beautiful. She was struck again by his strong jaw, his high cheekbones. He was handsome, there was no denying it. She did not know how to respond.

"You do not like it." Was she imagining it, or did he seem to be genuinely disappointed?

"No. It is not that," she said quickly. "I like it very much. It is just that, I did not expect to hear a song like that from a man like you."

"A man like me?"

"A warrior." Abigail knew she should not say the next part, but the words came out before she could stop them. "A man who saddles up and rides in the night with his men to slaughter the household of a man who insulted him."

David did not answer for a moment. He watched her.

"I see." Then he set the lyre aside. "Your bravery stopped me from doing something terrible," he finally said. "It was a mistake. A very bad one. My men were hungry, and I thought it was the only way to get them the food they needed. But I was trusting in my own power, and I was not trusting Yahweh to provide. I am grateful to you."

Abigail was surprised by his words. Was this a trick? Or was this warrior admitting that he'd made a mistake? Could he be truly grateful to her?

"I am grateful as well," Abigail said slowly. "Not just because my household was saved. But because when you take the throne as king over all of Israel, you will not have the blood of vengeance on your hands."

David ducked his head, nodding almost imperceptibly.

"The Lord has called you, and He will fight your battles," she continued. "And I believe that He will not let you be harmed, because He has called you for something greater."

"I hope you are right," was all he said in response. "Some days it is hard to trust."

She hesitated. She did not know how to respond to this.

"When you are king, please remember your servant," Abigail said.

David did not say anything for a moment. Then, quietly, he said, "I do not think I could forget you if I tried, Abigail."

Abigail blinked. His words made her feel things she had not felt in many years, since her early conversations with Ira. But she was not a child anymore. She was married, and he was... Well, he was David. She turned away. It was time to head back.

"Thank you, my lord. I wish you and your men great health." She started to walk. But as soon as she moved, David spoke again.

"How is your husband?"

"What?"

She turned back.

"He was ill. Has he recovered?"

"How did you know he was ill?"

"We know everything that goes on in these hills." David raised his chin just a little. A challenge, or an acknowledgment. And for some reason, she did not doubt his words, though she did not understand how it was possible.

"He has not recovered. He gets worse."

"I am sorry to hear it."

"Thank you." Then she turned back and started walking back up the hill toward the path once again. She could feel his eyes on her as she neared the crest of the hill. As she walked back toward Elisheba and Aya and Asaph, who appeared glad to see her reemerge, she tried to keep the color from her cheeks and to make her face appear calm.

David was dangerous, she realized. But it was in a whole different way than she had previously thought.

CHAPTER NINE

On the ninth day of Nabal's illness, she began to despair. Nabal could take no food, not even soups and other liquids. If things did not change, he would starve to death.

That evening, there was the sound of horses. More merchants come for what they were owed, Abigail thought, and readied herself to borrow the key to the locked room again, but in a few moments Eliab escorted a stranger into their main hall. He was accompanied by four servants, strong men and armed. They no doubt were his bodyguards on the long journey.

The man bowed to Abigail. His hair and beard were mostly gray, and there was something familiar about the lines of his face.

"Good evening." As soon as she heard his voice, she knew who he was. There was a family resemblance, but the man's countenance reflected concern rather than arrogance, so she had missed it at first. "I am Gerah, Nabal's brother. I received your message and came as soon as I was able."

Abigail bowed and studied the man before her. His eyes were kind and his bearing did not appear threatening.

"Thank you for coming, my lord. I am Abigail, your brother's wife. May I offer refreshments to you and your men after your long journey?"

Eliab and Yelena appeared, carrying cups of wine and some bread and fruit.

Gerah looked at the food. "Yes, thank you. But if you would see to my men, I would first like to see my brother."

"I will take you to him. His condition has not changed for nearly ten days. I have tried to give him nourishment, but he cannot respond or swallow. I fear he cannot last much longer without food."

Gerah nodded and turned to his men, indicating they were to partake of the food, and then he followed Abigail to Nabal's room.

He looked down at the still figure of his brother. Nabal's breathing was shallow, and his face had taken on a pallid look. Gerah leaned down and put a hand on Nabal's shoulder. He shook it slightly. "Nabal, it is Gerah. I am here." There was no response.

"I am sorry that we are meeting for the first time under such circumstances," Abigail said.

"As am I." Gerah did not take his eyes off his brother. "My brother has been an angry man for so many years. He would have nothing to do with the family."

She frowned. "What was the source of his anger?" It was an impertinent question, she knew, but she was getting used to speaking her mind freely. "He only mentioned once, when drunk with wine, that he had a family and where you lived, or I would not have known where to send word."

Gerah stroked his brother's arm gently. "Nabal was not favored by my father, even as a child. His birth cost our mother's life. I was a great deal older, and as the eldest son, our father's wealth would be left to me. Nabal believed he was being treated unfairly. My father and brother argued, and Nabal vowed he would make his own fortune. He was given his portion of the estate by our father, but with the help of some of our less reliable servants, somehow made off with a number of our father's sheep and goats. Our father was grieved but did not pursue him."

Gerah looked around at the large room, the comfortable bed, and the many servants. "My brother evidently managed to increase the herds to the numbers he has today. He has kept his promise, I see."

"Did he ever restore his relationship with your father?"

"No." Gerah shook his head. "When our father was dying, despite our urgent pleas, he would not come. All correspondence from us has been ignored. I learned that he had married, but my family was not invited to the wedding."

"I'm sorry to hear that. I did not know." She looked back at Nabal. "He was…is…a difficult man."

Gerah nodded, still stroking his brother's arm. Then he regarded her thoughtfully. "If my brother does not recover, what will you do?"

She had not wanted to think about that prospect, but her practical nature had considered the matter.

Before she could speak, he asked, "Do you have children?"

She shook her head. "Our only child, a boy, died at birth. There are no others."

With no heir to inherit Nabal's fortune, it would pass to his family. As a woman, Abigail was not entitled to any of it. It did no good to contemplate the injustice of this. It was not a surprise to her that the world was not fair to women.

They both knew what was required in this case, but Gerah spoke, shaking his head.

"I am afraid I cannot do that part of kinsman-redeemer. I already have a large family of my own and land holdings which require my time."

Abigail could not help the feeling of relief that swept through her. She would not be forced to marry a man she did not know once again.

"Is there no other close relative?" Abigail held her breath.

"I am his only brother," Gerah said. He seemed to think she would be devastated by the news. "I am afraid there is no other close relative. I am truly sorry."

Abigail nodded, thinking.

"What will you do?"

She lifted her chin as she addressed the man before her. "My mother died when I was young, and my father will need my care as he grows older. I will go to him."

Gerah nodded. "Let us see what happens with my brother and determine our course from there. I fear he shall not recover in his present condition, but the Lord God may be merciful. I will sit by my brother's bedside. Get some rest. We will speak in the morning."

She nodded. "I will have refreshments sent up to you."

"Thank you." He pulled up a covered bench and settled himself by the side of the bed, studying Nabal's face. She turned away from the sadness in his eyes. She could not share it.

She went down to the kitchen to oversee the evening meal and make sure the guards Gerah had brought were settled in quarters for the night and food was taken to them. She ate alone, but had no appetite and finally went up the stairs to her room.

All five of her maidservants were waiting.

"How is the master?" Talia asked.

"His condition has not changed."

Channah, her most tenderhearted maid, asked, "This brother, is he kind?"

"Yes, he is a good man. He is sitting with my husband through the night. I fear he is having a hard time seeing him this way after all these years."

Kai turned down her coverlet, and Yelena helped her pull off her clothes. Surely she could not bring them all back to Carmel. Her father's fortunes had been frittered away in the passing years, and she would not be able to inherit any of Nabal's fortunes. She wondered what she would do without these women. Life would be a lot lonelier.

When she finally bid her attendants good night and lay her head down on the pillow, she realized how weary she was in body and spirit. The strain was becoming hard to bear. How long would Nabal remain in this condition, and how long could Gerah stay? What would he do about Nabal's estate? She thought of the box of gold coins and considered when she should reveal it to Gerah. Only if Nabal died? She didn't mind returning to her father, for she loved the home she'd grown up in, but this had been her home for almost six years. Questions ran through her mind until she finally fell asleep out of exhaustion.

In the early hours of the morning, she was awakened by a cry. She recognized Nabal's voice. Gathering a robe around her, she rushed to his room. Gerah was staring down at his brother and turned to her, his face full of concern. He spread his hands in puzzlement.

"I don't know what to do for him. He suddenly awakened."

Nabal's eyes were open, and he was looking at something before him she could not see. Suddenly, as though struck by an unseen hand, he gasped and became lifeless.

Abigail knew in that moment that Nabal was gone.

CHAPTER TEN

Gerah stared down at his brother's body. "Something happened. I felt a presence in the room."

Abigail gazed at Nabal. There was no peace in his countenance. Even in death, his face remained angry. The man she had been married to for six years was dead.

She felt a sudden sense of relief, but then right away she felt guilty for the thought. She was now penniless, a widow. The man who had pledged his life to her was gone. She knew she should feel sorrow for her husband, but instead she felt like she had been released from a bad dream. She composed her face carefully so as to conceal her feelings from Gerah, who was obviously suffering grief.

"I will call the servants, and we will prepare the body for burial," she said quietly. "There is a place in the far corner of the estate that is used for a burial ground. Two elderly servants and our son are buried there."

Nabal's body was removed from the bed and laid out on a cloth on the floor. It was covered with another light cloth and candles were lit next to the body. Abigail summoned the local people who sat with the dead. Nabal's body was then washed and wrapped in a plain linen shroud.

Abigail's father was sent for and he, along with Gerah and men from the town, carried Nabal's body on a large plank. Abigail tore her clothes, as did Gerah, as the sign of mourning, and they followed the bier with the body of Nabal to the burial ground. Because of his wealth and status in the community, professional mourners were called. They followed the bier, weeping and flinging dust into the air. Nabal was buried, and when Abigail and Gerah returned to the house, a neighbor had supplied the meal of condolence for the family; eggs, a symbol of life, and loaves of fresh bread. No wine or meat would be consumed that week. Then according to custom, the neighbor men would sit with Gerah, Abigail, and her father for ten days.

Gerah, as the male relative, said the prayer of mourning each day, and a candle of mourning was lit. It would be tended and burned for twenty-four hours during this time. Neighbors continued to prepare and bring food for the mourners. The cook continued to feed the servants and Gerah's men. The servants went about their duties and spoke in hushed tones. Their eyes, seeking Abigail's, were full of unspoken questions.

When ten days had passed, Abigail's father prepared to return home. "When you have done what you need to do and settled with Gerah, you must leave this house of sadness and return to me." His hair was nearly all gray now, and his left eye was becoming milky. He seemed to have aged rapidly in the past week.

"Thank you, Abba. I will come to you as soon as I can. There is much to do."

He nodded, embraced her, and then left.

Abigail had retrieved the key chain from Nabal's body, and now she and Eliab took Gerah to Nabal's private room. Gerah's eyes widened at the box of gold coins.

"My brother was a wealthy man."

"Yes, I believe that is true."

Gerah was now a wealthy man, Abigail thought. Surely he would be pleased by this turn of events.

"I did not know about this box of gold, and yet you showed it to me. You could have hidden it from me, and I would not have known. You are an honest woman."

She looked at him steadily. "The Lord God watches what we do. He discerns even the thoughts of the heart. It would not have gone unnoticed if I had withheld your fortune from you."

"My brother was not worthy of you."

Abigail did not answer.

Gerah smiled ruefully. "I am sorry I am unable to do the part of kinsman-redeemer for you."

"It is all right. I will not be sad to leave." Abigail found that she meant it. "When the thirty days of mourning have passed, I will gather my things and return to my father's house."

"You will return home with five hundred shekels in your purse."

Abigail was stunned. "I— But…"

"You were a faithful wife to my brother. I have no doubt his wealth grew immensely because of your care. It is my gift of thanks."

Abigail did not know what to say. It was too much. And yet, she could not refuse it. Finally, she managed to say, "Thank you."

Gerah nodded.

"You will need someone to oversee the house and property, the shepherds and field workers," Abigail finally said. "Do you know of someone?"

Gerah's brow wrinkled in thought. "Yes, my youngest son, Zelek, is capable and has handled my flocks and herds. He will be happy to oversee a home of his own. I will send for him and his family."

Abigail felt like a weight had been lifted from her shoulders. She would observe the thirty days of mourning for Gerah's sake and out of respect for the loss of a husband, but she would count the days until she could leave the house of Nabal behind forever.

She answered, "That is good. I'm sure the workers and servants will be glad to have someone in charge again."

He chuckled. "You are an admirable woman. I believe you have been a great help to my brother. I am not unaware that your life cannot have been easy. I will give you all the help I can."

"Thank you."

◆

Gerah did not hurry his departure as the thirty days drew to an end. He waited for his son to arrive and become acquainted with the running of the estate. Abigail wondered about Zelek's wife. How would she feel about moving out to Maon? Was she used to running her own house? Or, maybe, as the wife of the youngest son, had she lived in the main house? If so, she might be delighted to have an estate to run on her own. Abigail hoped she would be capable and could take over quickly.

Abigail put her maidservants to work cleaning and preparing Nabal's room for Zelek and his wife. Other quarters were prepared for the three children she understood they were bringing. Nabal's clothes were packed and taken to the village to give to the poor. She opened the wooden shutters to let the fresh air in, instead of the gloom that had pervaded the room when Nabal was alive. Now the atmosphere seemed different. She bowed her head. *Thank You, my Lord, for all You have given me and for the strength to do what I must.* For the first time, she sensed a sweet presence in the room that had formerly held such anguish. She looked around a moment more, then put the past aside. She would remain in her own room until it was time to leave, and then it would be available for Zelek's youngest child.

Soon, Gerah's son arrived. He was tall and ruddy in features, a well-built man who looked capable of handling men and animals. He was as pleasant as he looked, and it was a relief that Abigail did not have a man as surly as Nabal to deal with. He brought his wife, Huldah, and three children. The children were quiet and well behaved, waiting for their mother to speak.

"I am Huldah. My husband and I welcome the opportunity to help you at this time."

She seemed a pleasant woman. Not pretty, but her warm personality caused Abigail to feel she would fit well in the household. Abigail remembered when she had come into this home for the first time, and hoped that Huldah's time here would be more pleasant than Abigail's own.

Zelek bowed low to Abigail. "I am honored to be able to oversee your late husband's flocks and herds. My wife is a capable housekeeper and will work with your steward." Then he turned and introduced the children.

"This is Micah. He is twelve. And these are my daughters, Sarah, who is ten, and Dora, who is six."

Dora was just a little older than her son would have been, Abigail noted. Micah was tall for his age but thin. The girls looked around with obvious curiosity. When Talia was sent for to lead them to their quarters, they bowed respectfully to Abigail and followed Talia.

Huldah followed Eliab to inspect their room and settle their things. Channah and Yelena went along to help. Abigail hurried to the kitchen to verify the menu she'd chosen for her guests. A lamb had been roasted, and there was a bitter herb salad with watercress, fresh mint, dandelion greens, grape halves, and walnut pieces. Fresh dill had been added, and a dressing of olive oil, honey, cloves, and wine vinegar. Braised cucumbers were chopped, along with leeks and fresh dill, and cooked in butter and olive oil. There was fresh bread with a ground sesame seed dip, and for the children she'd planned date cakes.

As the adults gathered later for the evening meal, Huldah noted the food the servants brought in. As they began to eat, she smiled at Abigail.

"Your cook is very capable." It was obvious she was pleased. Abigail nodded. In spite of Nabal's stinginess, he'd liked his food and they ate well. She smiled at Huldah. "Tomorrow let us go over the household matters. I'm sure you will want to see my own accounts."

"Yes, thank you." Huldah rose to go and see to the children, who had eaten in the kitchen, and prepare them for bed.

After the meal, Abigail had Eliab bring in the accounts from Nabal's private room and they pored over the figures. As Gerah and Zelek discussed the flocks and herds, Abigail told them how many shepherds her husband kept.

Abigail added, "As you are aware, shearing time is over and the majority of the fleeces have already gone to the merchants who buy them each year." Abigail's father was among them. "I will give you their names. We have kept some of the fleece here in storage to spin into thread for weaving for our own needs. You will not have to deal with shearing until next year."

Zelek nodded. "We also have finished the shearing season in Kerioth. We will ride out to Carmel in the morning to get acquainted with the shepherds and the men who tend the fields."

Abigail glanced at Gerah and smiled. "Thank you. I know the men who work for us have been anxious to learn what is going to happen. You will be able to assure them of their continued work."

It was late when her maidservants prepared her to retire for the night. When she was alone at last, she thanked the Lord for all He had provided. She lay quietly, contemplating Zelek and his family.

She could go home soon. The household would be in good hands. Now she could only entrust her future to her God and wait on His plan for her, whatever that entailed.

❖

After a breakfast of bread, fruit, and cheese, Gerah and his son were eager to be on their way and ride to Carmel to become acquainted with the men who worked for Nabal. As the new overseer, Zelek wanted to assure them he would continue to employ them.

After they left, Abigail turned to Huldah. "It was my pleasure to help many of the families of the workers in every way I could. My husband did not find it necessary to pay them well. Perhaps you are willing to assume that task?"

Huldah's face lit up, and she nodded. "I will be most happy to do that. It is something I also have done."

Abigail spent the rest of the morning introducing Huldah to the servants and giving her a tour of the estate. Then they went into the town of Maon to introduce Huldah to the wives of their workers. Abigail was pleased with Huldah's reception, and her concern for the families seemed genuine.

"We are going to miss you, my lady," said the wives as they called on each home. Some of the women wept as they realized Abigail was going away. Over and over they told Huldah stories of Abigail's care when they were ill or had recently given birth.

The evening of the second day, Gerah and Zelek returned. Abigail met them as they dismounted from their horses. The men were obviously tired.

"How did you find the flocks and herds? Was there any problem with the men?"

Zelek shook his head. "No, in fact, they seemed relieved that someone was now in charge. I heard much about your husband." He hesitated. "I'm afraid it was not kind."

"It is all right. I am well aware of their feelings for my husband."

"I assured them they would be paid fair wages, and I believe I will have no problems with them."

Abigail suppressed a smile at the words "fair wages" and inclined her head in agreement. How pleasant to find Nabal's family to be nothing like him.

◆

Abigail was pleased at how Zelek's family fit into the household, as if they had always been there. She enjoyed the sound of children's voices in the halls and would often stop to listen to them. She stood at the window looking out on the garden below where Huldah's children were chasing each other. Huldah sat on a stone bench nearby, keeping watch. Abigail put her hand to her heart and felt the familiar heaviness steal over her. Would she ever marry again? Was she doomed to never have children of her own? Her eyes filled with sudden tears, and she brushed them away. Bowing her head, she prayed softly, *Oh God Who Sees Me, grant me strength. Order my days and help me serve You with all that I am. My future is in Your hands.*

Abigail had her servants begin preparing her things for her journey to Carmel, and Gerah also prepared to return home. He had stayed longer than he expected to and was eager to return home to his wife and family.

Abigail walked outside with him to where one of his bodyguards was holding the reins of Gerah's horse.

"Go with our God, my lord, and may He grant you safe travels back to your home."

Gerah reached out and took her hands. "It has been a pleasure finally meeting my brother's wife. He chose well, in spite of himself. You will be all right. I wish you the blessing of a husband and family in due time." He paused. "I have decided to give a gift to your father and have authorized Zelek to send him one hundred sheep and a hundred goats."

Abigail was startled. "This is indeed generous, my lord. He will be pleased with such a gift. You are most kind."

Gerah's grandchildren then crowded around him, tears in their eyes at his departure. He embraced each one. "I will be back to visit you soon."

He mounted his horse, gave a final wave, and rode out of the yard with his men.

Abigail and the family watched him until the riders were a speck in the distance, and then she turned to the children. "I'm sure the cook has some almond-stuffed dates in the kitchen. Perhaps you would like to go and see?"

The children's eyes lit up at the prospect of sweets, and they hurried into the house. Huldah smiled her thanks and followed them.

CHAPTER ELEVEN

❖

The thirty days of mourning had been days of subdued activity. The days had passed peacefully as the household settled into their tasks and the family of Zelek made themselves at home. Huldah was now firmly in charge with the staff and especially the cook, and she and Eliab were on good terms as together they planned provisions for the household.

Abigail had relinquished her reign on the household to Huldah and would leave the next day. She sat in the orchard contemplating the course her life had taken and praying for wisdom. She'd put her maidservants to work packing the items she indicated she would take and now needed a little time to herself.

The sun was warm on her shoulders as she watched a golden and black butterfly alight on a rose nearby. The garden had been her solace on difficult days, and when she prayed she felt the presence of her Lord.

With the spring and the barley harvest approaching, it would soon be time for Passover again. Huldah assured her that she would also celebrate with their workers, and Abigail was glad for her people.

There was the sound of horses and men's voices in the front of the house. Were these visitors for Zelek? When had he had the time to make alliances in the village? A few minutes later, Eliab came toward her, walking quickly, his face puzzled.

"My lady, there are some men here to see you. They have been sent by David."

Abigail rose. Were they in need of more food? "Did they say why they have come?"

"No, my lady, they wish to speak with you alone."

She entered the main room of the house to find five men standing respectfully, waiting for her. They were clothed in dingy robes and their hair and beards were untrimmed, but their presence commanded the room nonetheless. She recognized two of them as the men who had escorted her home that fateful night.

Huldah and Eliab stood by, watching Abigail. She remembered Eliab's words about how he would turn David in to Saul if given the chance.

She turned to the members of the household. "I will speak to them alone. It is all right."

They nodded and slowly left the room. Huldah looked back at Abigail, as if to remind her that she now handled the business for the household, but she left.

Abigail turned to the men. "How may I help you? Does your leader need more provisions? We would gladly send them."

One of the men suppressed a smile. He looked to the one who seemed to be in charge.

The man stepped forward and cleared his throat. "My lady, I am Abishai, a servant of David. It has come to his attention that your husband, Nabal, has died and you are now a widow."

"Yes."

"David has sent us on an important mission. He has waited through your time of mourning and now wishes you to come to him and be his wife."

Abigail stepped back. "His wife?"

"David was greatly impressed by your courage and favorable appearance," Abishai said.

Abigail wanted to laugh. Her courage and favorable appearance? Was that enough to choose a wife?

She had wondered if she would ever marry again, but she had not expected this. Not this quickly. Besides, David was married to Michal, the daughter of the king. She would be his second wife. Could she be willing to become a second wife?

But then, if she was honest with herself, she had not stopped thinking about David since they had met in the wilderness. He was mysterious, dangerous. He was a man who spent his days composing songs to the Lord, seeking Yahweh's heart, and his nights rampaging villages and killing all those within. He had been chosen by God to lead, but he was immature and ruled by his emotions. He was handsome. There was no denying that. She had already wondered, more than she would ever admit, what it would be like to be close to him and feel the strength of his arms around her.

It made no sense. A respectable woman like her, a widow of a wealthy man in good standing, could not marry the man leading the rebellion against the king. It would be madness. All the things Nabal had said about David and his men rushed through her head. Ruffians. Rebels. Traitors.

But Samuel had said differently. The prophet had said that David had been chosen by God to rule Israel.

David was wild, complicated, exciting. He was faithful and strong and handsome. He was everything Nabal was not.

Abigail was aware that the men were watching her, but she did not move. She continued to let her mind run through the possibilities.

Being a second wife was better than having no husband at all. It would mean children, and purpose. She could bear the son of the king of Israel. Would her own child someday rule?

But if that were to come to pass, it would be very far in the future. For now, if she said yes to David, she would live in a camp in the wilderness, always on the run. After managing her own household, sleeping on a soft bed, and eating fine foods, how could she move to a tent and beg for food? Could she live day by day, knowing that her life was in danger?

Then again, was that any worse than the stifling sameness of the life she'd lived with Nabal?

The men were watching her, waiting for her answer.

Did she really have a choice? Women did not make such decisions; men decided marriage. But somehow, Abigail knew this was different. She was not a young maiden now. She was older, more experienced. She was a wealthy woman. She could decide to ignore the customs of her culture if she so chose.

And she could not deny that her heart had already chosen.

Beyond that, she could not help but feel that she was *supposed* to say yes now. She felt, in the strangest way, that God wanted her to be a part of this. She had the sense that He would use her somehow to build the kingdom of Israel. He had given her this opportunity, and she felt in a way she could not explain or begin to understand that He wanted to her to say yes and become a part of something much bigger than herself.

"Yes," she said. "I will marry David."

Abishai smiled, then he turned to his men and they spoke among themselves a moment. "If it pleases you, my lady, we will camp here. We are to bring you with us when we return tomorrow."

Tomorrow?

"So soon? I will need to make arrangements."

"I am afraid there is not much time. David has already stayed longer in the area than he intended, waiting for your days of mourning to end."

He had waited for her. She could not help the smile that rose up.

"We will have our steward make arrangements for food and quarters," Abigail said.

She called Eliab, who she knew would be waiting nearby, and also Huldah. A servant was sent to bring Zelek in from the fields. He came quickly.

"Is something wrong?"

"There has been a change in my plans, Zelek. I shall not be returning to my father's house after all. The men came from David with a request that I come to him and be his wife."

Huldah gasped. "His wife?"

Abigail was not surprised by her shock. It was a stunning turn of events.

"How do you know David? Isn't he a fugitive from the king?" Zelek's brow furrowed with concern.

"Would that not be dangerous?" Eliab added. He did not approve of David, but she knew this question came from another place. Eliab had been her husband's faithful steward, but he had grown to trust Abigail too, and she was touched to see his concern for her now. "What do you know of this band of outlaws?"

She told them the story—which Eliab already knew—of the men who had come to Nabal and his response. Then she related how she had saved her husband's household by meeting David and his men as they were riding toward the estate. She shook her head. "The shock of my news was evidently too much for Nabal's heart. That's when he fell ill and became as your father found him."

Zelek took the news in without any outward sign that he understood. Abigail pressed on, explaining how she had run into David in the valley on the way to Carmel.

Zelek listened, and then he said, "You are a wealthy woman now. It will bring David much good to be allied with someone like you."

Abigail felt like she'd been slapped across the face. Was that what he thought? That David was marrying her for her money? But how would David even know Gerah had given her such a large amount of gold?

Then she remembered David saying he knew everything that went on in the hills in this area. Could he have heard about this as well?

Was David marrying her for her money? The thought had not occurred to her. She was certain that he'd felt what she'd felt on that hillside. That pull that had made it seem almost impossible that they would not come together one way or another. But could Zelek be right?

"You are also beautiful," Huldah said quickly, as though to erase the sting of her husband's words. "I am not at all surprised that he was taken with you."

"You have answered him favorably?" Zelek asked, ignoring his wife's words.

She nodded.

"They say he is very handsome," Huldah said. "And that he will be the next king."

"But Saul is the king now," Eliab said. "You would live your life as the wife of a fugitive. What would you do if David were killed? You and the others in his camp could be killed also. You must think of this."

She knew he was trying to protect her. But her mind was made up. Something deep inside her knew that this was right. That someday, David would be king, and that she would have a role to play in his kingdom. Perhaps she would bear him the son who would rule after him.

"I have thought of it," she said. "But I trust that Yahweh will preserve and protect the one He has chosen."

Zelek was silent for a moment, and then, almost reluctantly, he said, "You must send word to your father."

Then she remembered Gerah's gift. "Do you wish me to have the sheep and goats your father sent to my home returned?" She did not mention the gold, though she knew he knew about that as well.

He raised his eyebrows. "My father wished to thank you. It is all yours to keep."

"Thank you, Zelek. You are more than generous."

"May you go in peace, Abigail, in the will of the Most High. I will send provisions with you, and also at any time you have need of them. Just send me word."

"Thank you. I'm sure David and his followers will be grateful."

Huldah smiled wanly. "We send our blessings on your new life. May you bear David sons."

Abigail hoped for the same thing. After bowing to her nephew, she hurried to her room to give instructions to her five maidservants. Her life with David would be very different from her life with Nabal. She would take only the clothes she thought necessary. She would send the rest of the items she'd packed to her father. She wrote a letter telling him of her decision. Her father would be disappointed, but she knew he would resign himself. Maybe even be glad for her.

Anna gave orders to the other four maidservants, and they raced to do all that was needed. Clothes were quickly separated into piles as Abigail pointed to the items she wanted to take and those she couldn't. As they packed, her maidservants watched her anxiously. She still had not said anything about what would happen to them. She hoped they would be willing to come with her, but she did not know what they would say. Any who did not wish to come with her, she would send home to her father's house.

"You know of my decision to go to David and become his wife," she finally said when they were all gathered.

Anna spoke up. "Mistress, we have long been with you. We wish to go wherever you go."

Abigail sighed. "The circumstances will not be the same. You would not serve in a great house. David is a fugitive from Saul, and his camp must move frequently. Would you be willing to live like that?"

Anna glanced around at the other four maidservants, who all nodded their assent.

"You will need us, mistress. We will go."

Overcome by emotion, Abigail embraced each of the women. They were more like family to her than servants. All but Kai had been with her since her youth in her father's house, and thankfully they were still loyal to her.

Then they had begun the repacking in earnest and the women prepared their own things in traveling bags.

David's men had been fed and housed, and the next morning as the sun began to rise on the horizon, Abigail and her maids finished packing. She had slept, but only for a short time, as her mind turned with what was to happen this day.

She tucked the bag that contained her gold into a satchel to bring with her. She also took her headband of gold coins she had saved in a carved wooden box. She had brought no furniture to the marriage, so she would take none now. But she wavered over bringing her loom and skeins of wool. It would be difficult to carry all that from place to place, but finally she decided to take it. The servants strapped it onto one of the donkeys. She hoped David would not think her foolish to bring such a thing when they had to move quickly.

The day was getting warm, though it was still early morning. David's men were anxious to leave. Zelek had provided a cart, which was cleaned and would provide transportation for her five maidservants. Another cart was found to transport the things Abigail was sending to her father.

Huldah capably arranged for the food and provisions Abigail would bring with her. She looked over the loaded donkeys. "You will not go to your new husband empty-handed, my lady."

The staff, along with Zelek and Huldah, stood silently to watch her go. She had spoken to each one and thanked them for their service to her. Tears flowed from the eyes of many of them.

Huldah took her hand. "May the Lord God go with you, Abigail."

"Remember my word to send other provisions if you need them," added Zelek. "David will be king of Israel one day as the prophet Samuel has said. May you be blessed as his wife."

Abigail thanked Zelek for his blessing and offer, then looked around at what had been her home for almost six years. The buildings held no nostalgia for her.

As the procession finally moved forward, Abigail turned her eyes toward the mountains and the man who awaited her. She did not look back.

❖

As the sun began to rise over the mountains at midday, Abigail and her caravan approached the camp. She looked for David and soon saw him standing in front of the members of his camp, who had all gathered to welcome them.

When she saw him, her heart clenched. He was as handsome as she had remembered, but who was he? She did not know this man. Would he be kind? Had she chosen well?

But as they approached, she saw a smile spread across his face. And also—was that relief? She realized that he had not known whether she would come, and tenderness rose inside her. She saw that this brave warrior, this future king, had been worried that she might reject his offer.

"Abigail."

The sound of his voice made her insides feel warm.

"You have come." He stepped forward and, when she was close, he lifted her off her donkey.

She could not help the shriek that came out of her. She immediately covered her mouth. She was not some young girl in the market, but David laughed. His arms were strong around her, and she felt secure.

"Yes, my lord. I am glad to accept your proposal."

Their eyes held for a moment, and Abigail once again felt that spark that she had felt on that hillside.

David set her down and gave orders for the men to help her unload her belongings. Then he looked over at the five maidservants she had brought with her. His brows rose.

"They would not be left behind," Abigail quickly explained. "They have been with me most of my life."

"We will make a place for them." He nodded. "Welcome to our camp."

Abigail looked out over the haphazard collection of animal-skin tents and stores of food and belongings. Cooking smoke rose up from among the tents, and goats and sheep wandered between them. Everything seemed to be coated in a layer of mud. She met Anna's eyes and saw that Anna was thinking along the same lines she was: this was going to be very different than what they were used to.

She then told David Zelek's words about additional provisions and what he had sent with her. His eyes widened. "Truly the Lord God is generous. All you have brought is greatly needed. I will send my thanks when my men return the donkeys."

He looked at her and seemed to forget the words he had been about to speak. She felt a warmth spread through her.

"Ahinoam, please show Abigail to her tent," he finally said, keeping his eyes on her. "You may settle in and refresh yourself."

"Thank you." She ducked her head, but he kept his gaze on her, a look she could not read on his face.

David's officers then began to come forward and greet her, including his brothers, who had joined him, along with their families, to escape retribution from Saul.

Abigail met so many people she could not keep their faces straight, and David seemed to sense that. He stepped forward and murmured, "You will meet them all in time. Let Ahinoam show you to your tent." Then, after a moment, he added, "You will have to share it with your maidservants."

"I expected as much. It is fine. We will adapt to whatever we need to," Abigail said.

David nodded. "Refresh yourself, and I will be waiting for our celebration."

Even as he spoke, she could see that preparations were underway to make use of the food she had brought.

Abigail and her servants followed the woman through the squalid camp, threading between cooking fires and earthenware jugs and carts piled haphazardly in the narrow aisles between the tents. Abigail caught several people turning to catch a glimpse of her as they made their way to the large tent David had set up for her.

"Welcome to our camp. I am Ahinoam," the woman said as they walked. "Also David's wife."

Abigail's foot missed the ground, and she grabbed on to Yelena to right herself. "What?"

"His wife." There was no rancor in her face, only the statement of a fact.

"I…did not realize he had another wife," Abigail said. She had known about Michal, of course. But Michal was not here. He had not mentioned… But then he hadn't really spoken to her about much of anything, really.

She would be David's third wife, then. It was not all that different from being his second wife, she reasoned; but somehow, it felt different.

Ahinoam was young, Abigail realized. Younger than Abigail, but plain, with a body that was slim like a young boy's. Abigail hated the flash of satisfaction that coursed through her.

Ahinoam nodded. Abigail couldn't read the look on her face. Was that animosity? She seemed to be looking right past Abigail at something beyond her. How could she not be upset? Abigail could not imagine that Ahinoam would be indifferent to David taking another wife. But what could she do? What could either of them do? She wanted to explain that she had not known, that she had no choice, that they were both in the same situation, but she could not get the words to come out.

"I'm glad to meet you," Abigail finally said. "I look forward to working together." It was the best she could do.

Ahinoam bowed her head, keeping her eyes averted, and stepped back. "I will leave you here."

Abigail thanked her and pulled back the heavy hide flap. Inside, there was a stack of mats, as well as blankets and a few cooking pots.

Abigail looked around and shook her head. "Life is going to be quite different." Yelena and Channah stepped in behind her, followed by Kai and Talia and Anna.

"It will be cozy," Anna said, her voice just a touch too bright.

Abigail did not have much time to think about her new living conditions, though, as water was brought and she was able to wash off the dust of her travels. Anna helped her into a soft blue tunic with gold trim. She had brought this one dress for her wedding, but the rest of her clothes were plain, to work and travel in. Her hair was dressed and once more the ring of coins was placed on her forehead. Scented oil was rubbed into her skin. There was no veil, but these were different circumstances from her first wedding. As long as she became David's wife, it did not matter.

When she was ready, Anna led her to David, who stood in front of his tent. Rugs were placed on the ground and someone had gathered wildflowers to place around the rugs. David had also refreshed himself and changed into a robe made of fine linen, embroidered with gold thread. His beard was trimmed and his hair brushed back from his face. Abigail felt her breath leave her lungs. He was the most handsome man she'd ever seen. She could not believe she was to become his wife.

Everyone from the camp gathered around them, and when all eyes were upon them, David took Abigail's hand and looked out over the gathered assembly. "Be it known this day that I have taken Abigail of Maon to me as my wife. She will be treated with the same respect you have given me. Let us rejoice and celebrate this great occasion."

The dressed lambs Abigail brought had been roasted, the rice cooked with herbs, and the fava beans cooked and then fried with olive oil and cumin seeds. There were no fresh greens, but she'd brought goat cheese mixed with olives. Also, she had packed all the date cakes from her storage room and the women cut them in small portions so everyone could have a taste. The wineskins were hung on poles, and the wine flowed. Someone began to play a flute, and several women brought out their tambourines and began to dance. Some of the men formed a line and danced to the music, as the others clapped in response. David took her hand and danced with her, abandoning himself to the joy of the music.

The celebration went on for hours, but finally, calling out their good wishes, women slipped away to tend sleepy children. Men tended to the animals and joined their families. Abigail's maidservants began to help some of the women of the camp clean up the remains of the celebration. Anna looked at her mistress, a question in her eyes.

Abigail quietly nodded her head, and Anna stood back.

The evening star twinkled as David turned to Abigail and lifted her to her feet. As she stood, she caught a glimpse of Ahinoam, who quickly looked away, but not before Abigail had seen the look of sadness on her face. Ahinoam occupied herself with putting food into wooden containers.

"Come, Abigail," David said softly. He took her hand and led her to his tent. His hand was warm, his skin flushed from dancing. He lifted the tent flap and pulled her inside, and then let the flap fall closed before he stepped closer to her and touched his fingers to her cheek, gently. Her skin tingled under his touch.

"You are so beautiful," he said, his voice husky. He let his fingers trail down her cheek and onto her neck, caressing her skin gently. Abigail held her breath. Every part of her was alive.

Softly, so gently she did not realize at first, he pulled on the sash of her gown, untying it. He stepped closer and studied her for a moment before he leaned forward and kissed her. His kisses went from soft and gentle to hungry, and she had never felt the rush of emotions that threatened to overtake her. Eventually, when he laid her down gently on his mat, she understood that in David's hands, this wedding night would be very different than her first.

CHAPTER TWELVE

David fulfilled her bridal week, and the camp left them alone as much as was possible. Abigail had never known pleasure like she'd found with David, and she longed to be with him every moment, even when he had to leave the tent for short times. His men brought them meals, and they lounged in the tent, enjoying fresh bread and honey and cheese and delicious wine.

"I wish it could be like this forever," David said one night as they lay on the mats, tangled up together in a light blanket. "The two of us, and no one else."

"Let's make it so," Abigail said. "We could run away together, just the two of us. We'll find a small patch of land near a stream and live there alone, where no one can find us."

"It sounds wonderful." His fingertips traced along the inside of her arm, raising goose bumps along her flesh. "We will make love all day, and sleep all night."

"We will have many sons," Abigail said. "More than we can count."

"No one will bother us." David pushed himself up on his elbow, his fingers running gently up and down her skin. "We will have no responsibilities. Nothing to fear."

Abigail slid her arm underneath him and pulled him close. "I do not fear anyone as long as you are near."

David bent his neck and let his lips hover over hers. "Soon, very soon, you will not have to fear anyone at all."

"What do you mean?" She knew that Yahweh would crown David king is His own time. But they had never spoken of this being a certainty in the near future.

"I am tired of waiting, tired of hiding out and hoping the king will not find us," David said. His breath was warm against her skin. "I do not want to spend my life hiding. That is not what a king does. This life"—he used his free hand to gesture around the tent—"this is not what you deserve. You should be living in a palace, surrounded by marble and fresh water and clean linens." He brushed his lips across hers, gently. "When I am king, you will have the finest clothes, and you will eat lamb every day and drink the most delicious wines."

"That sounds wonderful." His skin was soft and warm, but his muscles were hard under her fingers. "But I do not need fine clothes and wines. All I need is to be with you."

"You will be with me always," David said. "I will not let you out of my sight. Once I am king, you will be with me every moment." He kissed her again, deeper this time. "Soon."

"Has Yahweh told you how?" David heard from the Lord more clearly than anyone she knew. His heart was so aligned with Yahweh, and he sought the Lord's counsel so often, that David seemed to know God's thoughts as well as he knew his own.

"I have a plan." He stroked his fingers down the side of her body, and Abigail nearly lost herself in the sensation, but she could not let herself give in. Something stuck in her mind. She realized that he had not answered her question.

"What did Yahweh tell you to do?"

"I will overtake Saul," David said. "He has more men, and he is more powerful, but I am more clever."

"How will you do that?"

"Saul and his army are arranging themselves in battle against the Philistines. He is distracted," David said. "He believes I fear him, and he will not expect me to show up where he is." He kissed her, gently. "I will go to him, and get him alone."

Abigail did not mean to pull back, but she felt herself move away just a bit. "Your plan is to shed the blood of the king?"

David pulled her closer and put her mouth next to her ear. "The Lord has told me that *I* will be king."

His breath was warm and his voice deep, and he moved his hand to stroke the soft skin of her stomach. She wanted to let herself give in, to think about this all later. But instead, she asked, "But is this the way for you to ascend to the throne?"

David did not move for a moment, though his body tensed. She could feel his heart beating against hers. "Do you not believe in me?" he asked quietly.

"On the contrary, my lord. I gave up everything to come with you because I believe you are the one Yahweh has called." Her words seemed to placate him some, but he still held still. "I am not questioning the Lord's call. I am only asking about the timing."

"I am tired of waiting." His voice had taken on an edge. He was a man who was used to getting what he wanted; Abigail had already come to understand this.

"I understand." She used a soothing voice, and she ran her fingers gently up and down his back. "I cannot wait for the day when you will sit on the throne. But if the Lord has promised it, is it not His duty to bring it about?"

"Perhaps this is the way He is doing so. Maybe He has given me strength and resources so that I will be positioned to remove the king now."

Abigail paused to choose her words carefully. She did not feel confident that her husband was choosing the right path, but she knew she could not come out and say so plainly. The only words that came to her were the ones her father had used with her so many times.

"Have you asked Yahweh whether this is the right course of action?"

David did not say anything but pulled back and shifted his position so he lay next to her.

She did not want to push him, but she felt she must. "Do you really believe it is Yahweh's plan for you to shed the blood of the Lord's anointed?"

His hand rested on her belly, but it remained still.

"What Yahweh has promised, He will bring to pass." Abigail pushed herself up on her elbow now and leaned over him. Her long hair fell over her face and brushed his chest. "It is our place to seek His guidance and to continue to trust. He will be faithful, no matter how long it takes."

For a brief moment, she wanted to laugh at the fact that she was the one urging caution. Her father would not believe that his lessons all these years had actually sunk in. But David was listening, she could see. He was not happy to hear her words, but he was considering them.

She watched him for a moment, seeing his chest rise and fall. She let her eyes trace the lines of his face, the strong curve of his jaw, his well-muscled shoulder. She still could not believe this man was her husband. That she got to be united with him always.

"You will sit on the throne someday," she said. "And it will be beautiful, because the Lord God will have brought it to pass. His hand will bring it to pass, not your own."

He was looking up toward the ceiling of the tent, but he was listening. She placed her hand on his chest.

"You will rule with honor, because you are aligned with Yahweh. His presence will be felt."

A slight smile curved his lips now.

"What is that smile for?"

"I have been thinking of an idea," David said. "You just reminded me about it."

"What is that?"

"When I am king, I want the Lord's presence to be housed with me, literally."

Abigail sucked in a breath. She knew exactly what he meant. "The Ark of the Covenant?"

The Ark was the most holy article of their faith. The dwelling place of the Most High. It had been stored in Keriath Jearim, in the house of a man called Abinidab, since it had been recovered from the Philistines.

David nodded, his hair brushing against the mat beneath him. "When I am king of Israel, I will bring it to my palace so that all will know the God we serve."

Once he said the words, they seemed so obvious that she could not believe she had not thought of it herself. Of course the Ark of the Covenant should be housed in the palace of Israel's king. David would bring it to pass.

"Brilliant," she said. "All the more reason to wait for God's timing."

And then she leaned over and kissed him, letting her weight fall on him. It took him a moment to respond, still lost in contemplation, but then he seemed to come back to the present, and he began to run his hands over her body hungrily. He pulled her to him and kissed her deeply.

He would think about her words later, she was certain. But for the moment, neither of them thought of anything but their desire for one another.

◆

When it was time for Abigail to return to her own tent, Anna met her with a smile.

"You are happy, mistress," Anna said, a knowing look in her eye.

"Yes, Anna. I am." She had not known that the marriage bed could be like this, and she had left David's tent sure there would be a child growing in her belly soon.

Anna helped her bathe and change her garments. Yelena, Talia, and Channah had carried jugs of water from a nearby stream for her bath and heated them on the fire, and she thanked them for their efforts.

While she had been gone, her loom had been set up in a corner of the tent, and though it made things more crowded, she was anxious to work on it again. But there was much to do in the camp. She had asked David for permission to make some changes so things were more organized. She could see ways to make it easier to keep clean and to pack up quickly if they had to move, and he had given her free reign. She wanted to bring order so when they had to move camp suddenly to avoid Saul, it was not a frantic gathering of supplies and possessions. There was too much chance of leaving some items behind.

As she contemplated where to begin, Channah came quietly to stand before her.

"Yes, Channah?"

Channah did not speak much, but Abigail knew her soft brown eyes missed little. After a moment's hesitation, she shared what was on her mind.

"Mistress, you have five of us to take care of you, but without the large home we have left behind, things have changed. We are crowded here, but your master's other wife has no one to help her. Might I be released to serve her?"

"Bless your kind heart, Channah, for seeing what I could not see. I didn't realize that." Channah was right. Why did Abigail need five servants when David's other wife had none? She put a hand on her servant's shoulder. "If that is your wish, I am glad to have you help Ahinoam. Go with my blessing."

Channah beamed. "Thank you, mistress. I will serve her as I served you." She gathered her few things and left the tent.

Talia, who had entered with a water pot, watched her go. "Ahinoam has watched the bridal tent all week, mistress. She is sad."

Abigail contemplated her words. She had tried not to think about the woman she shared her husband with. She couldn't imagine that his time with Ahinoam was anything like what she and David experienced. But it would not do any good to pretend she did not exist. They must live together, whether she liked it or not. "It is time I called on her."

◆

As Abigail approached Ahinoam's tent, the younger woman's face betrayed no emotion. She neither smiled in welcome nor gave any hint that she resented Abigail. Only her eyes, like dark pools, showed her pain.

Abigail reached out a hand. "Ahinoam, let there be no discord between us. I come in friendship."

Ahinoam gestured for her to step inside the tent but did not rise from her mat. Abigail came in and let the tent flap fall closed behind her.

"We will help David most if we work together," Abigail said.

Ahinoam nodded but did not say more. The air fairly crackled with the tension between the women.

Abigail tried to find the words to say what she wanted to convey. She hesitated, and then finally she said, "I did not know."

It was not an apology, exactly. Neither of them had done wrong. But it seemed to soften Ahinoam's countenance some.

"Would it have changed your answer if you had known?" Ahinoam asked.

Abigail thought for a moment, and then she shook her head. "No," she said. She could be nothing but honest. "It would not have changed my answer."

Ahinoam nodded, as if she'd already known what Abigail would say. "I did know about Michal," she said softly. "And it did not change my answer."

She loved him too, then. They had that in common.

"Does he ever see her?" Abigail asked.

"No." Ahinoam shook her head, and her dark curls swung around her shoulders. "I was told that when David became a fugitive, Michal was given by her father to another man. It grieved David for a long time." She looked down at the dirt floor. "He married me...after."

Abigail wished to know more about the circumstances of their marriage, how long they'd been married and what had made him choose her. But she knew she could not ask. Not yet. Instead, she looked around. Ahinoam's tent was larger than her own and not as full. It was just her in here, plus Channah, and she did not have a loom or the clothes Abigail had brought with her.

"You sent Channah to help me," Ahinoam said. "For that I thank you."

"I am glad to do it," Abigail said. The words relieved a bit of the tension, but there was still an awkwardness between them. Abigail had hoped that they could become friends, but she was seeing now how foolish that was. "I hope we can get along and work together to serve the man we both love."

Ahinoam did not look at her.

Over the next few days, under David's orders, Abigail met many of the other women of the camp and did her best to bring order to the way the supplies were stored and to clean up the look of the camp. The other women were friendly, and most were interested in getting to know this new woman who had entered David's life and his camp. New supplies arrived every few days from Zelek, and life quickly settled into an easy rhythm. She cleaned, cooked, and kept the camp in order during the day, and she spent the nights in David's bed. She noted, with more than a little satisfaction, that he did not call for Ahinoam at all that first month. He only had eyes for Abigail, and she welcomed his attentions and delighted in his touch.

She did not ask where David went during the day or where his men got the supplies they often returned to camp with. David had not mentioned attacking Saul again, for which she was glad. She was in no rush for him to become king. Things were going along just fine as they were now.

CHAPTER THIRTEEN

The heat of the summer was fully upon them when a young man staggered into camp, held up by two of David's men. David had been meeting with several of his top advisors, but the cries from the men at the edge of the camp summoned them all. Abigail also ran to see what the commotion was, followed by Ahinoam and several of the other women. Abigail saw that the newcomer was frightfully thin and dirty, and his hair had grown too long. He was wearing rags, and it took her a moment to realize that they were the remains of a priest's ephod.

"We were on our way back from getting supplies from Maon when we found him along the road," a man named Meshullam explained. "His donkey had given out and collapsed."

"Give him water and some fruit," David ordered, and the people scattered to do what David had asked. They held the skin of water to his mouth and watched as he drank thirstily. When he had rested and collected himself, David asked him to explain himself.

"I am grateful I found you. I have been searching for many weeks."

"Why were you looking for us?" David asked.

"You are my only hope. If Saul finds me, I am a dead man."

"Who are you, and what happened?" David asked.

"I am Abiathar, son of the high priest, Ahimelech."

Abigail sucked in a breath. She had heard the story, back when Nabal was still alive. Eliab had told her; it had been his excuse for not sharing food and supplies with David's men. But when she looked at David, she could see that he did not know what had happened after his visit to Nob.

"I am from the city of priests. You came to our city to ask for bread."

David nodded. "I remember. Your people were generous. Your father gave me the sword of Goliath as well as bread for our people. We are grateful."

"My father did not know that you had fallen out with King Saul. When he helped you, he thought you were there on a mission from the king."

David's face clouded. Abigail could see that he was starting to guess where this man's story was leading.

"Doeg the Edomite was there in Nob, and he saw what my father did," Abiathar said. He brushed his too-long hair back from his face. "Doeg went to Saul and told him that he'd seen my father helping you. The king was furious. He ordered the priests to come before him and explain. My father tried to explain that he didn't know you were running from the king. My lord, you were the king's greatest warrior."

Abigail knew what happened next, but she did not want to hear the words. It would somehow make them real.

"What did Saul do?" David asked.

"Saul had the Edomite kill my father. Then he ordered him to kill all eighty of the priests standing there." A sob escaped from Abiathar's throat, and he could barely choke out the words. "Then the king ordered the Edomite to slay every priest in our town, also the women, children, and animals. Everyone."

Several of the people in hearing gasped. "The king has gone mad," someone whispered.

David's face showed no emotion, but a muscle worked in his jaw.

The young man began to weep. "My mother, my sisters, and my little brother. All run through with a sword."

Raya, the wife of Joab, who was standing nearby, handed the man a cloth with which to wipe his eyes.

"I am so sorry," David said. "It is unthinkable that helping me led to this."

Abiathar nodded, swiping the cloth under each eye.

"How did you manage to escape?" David asked.

"I hid in the corridor and snuck out through the sewers," Abiathar said, choking back tears. "I know I should have stood and fought, but I—"

"You did well," David said, taking a step toward him. "If you had tried to fight, you would be dead, along with the others. I am glad you have escaped, and you are welcome here. You will be safe with us. I will protect you with my life, for the same person wants to kill us both." David reached out and touched his shoulder gently. "How did you find us?"

"I made it as far as Carmel and was told by several people where to find your camp," Abiathar said.

"We have stayed too long in one place if many people know where we are," David said. "It is my fault. I have been distracted."

He did not say what had distracted him, but the knowing looks that passed between the men made it clear they all knew what—who—he was referring to. Abigail felt her cheeks flame. Was she nothing more than a distraction, then?

David commanded the men to bring Abiathar to a tent and to treat his wounds, and then David went out to the wilderness alone, his lyre tucked under his arm. Abigail knew that he had gone to spend time talking to God, asking for direction, begging for wisdom.

Abigail returned to her tent and did her best to comfort her maidservants, who were whispering together in the tent when she arrived. She knew they were all afraid that Saul would find them and mete out vengeance on their camp, as he had the city of priests.

"We are in the hand of our God." Abigail hoped she sounded more confident than she felt. "David will be king because the prophet has anointed him. God will not let anything happen to David or to us."

The words brought her comfort, and she prayed they were true. She had chosen this life and had known that she was risking danger. But she could not change things now. She could only trust in God's promise that David would be the next king.

David did not call for her that night, or for Ahinoam. She heard him crying out to God, late into the night. The lantern was still lit in his tent when Abigail finally fell asleep.

◆

At first light, David gave the command to pack up the carts and move out. They were in danger here. They were all moving a short time later and walked until they had entered a heavily forested area on the outskirts of Ziph. They set up their camp, but Abigail could see that David remained unsettled. Something had changed in his countenance. He still called for her most nights, but he seemed distracted, his actions rote, his mind elsewhere.

"You are preoccupied," she said one night as she pulled her robe around her. He was lying on the mat, staring up at the ceiling.

"I am sorry." He let out a sigh and rolled to his side to face her. "I am responsible for the safety of all of these people. It is a great responsibility, and it weighs on me."

An oil lamp cast flickering shadows over his face, and she saw that there were dark crescents under his eyes.

"The people of Ziph will not give us up," Abigail said. The residents of the town, at least those on the edges, had to know they were here, but so far they had left the camp alone.

"I fear they will. Surely they have heard word of what happened at Nob."

"There must be a way to find out," Abigail said.

"My brother Abinadab is to ride into town in the morning and ask around."

"What will he do? Ride into the city and ask whether the people want to kill us?" Abigail tied the sash of her robe.

"I do not know." David let out a sigh. "Maybe it is better to simply keep moving. If we stay too long in one place, we are bound to be discovered anyway."

"It would be better to stay longer if we can," Abigail said. Being constantly on the move was very trying for the women and children, and there were several women who were nearing their time. It would be nearly impossible for them to deliver their babies while the camp was on the move, and they could not leave them behind.

"Then we must send someone into town to see what is being said, to find out whether they know about us," David said.

Abigail could see his logic, but she did not see how Abinidab could do this job. The men in this camp all had a look. Abinidab was dirty, as all David's men were, and wore ragged clothes. None of them had shaved in some time. "Surely they will know that he is one of us. He will give us away for sure."

"There is no other way to know what is being said in town."

Abigail sat on the edge of the mat for a moment, thinking. Surely it was madness. He would never allow her to…

And yet she knew she could do the job in a way that would not give their position away.

"What if there was another way?"

❖

Abigail walked into the market in Ziph the next day, followed by Anna and Yelena, and for a moment, it almost felt like they were back in Carmel, gathering supplies for her father's meal.

But this time, there was much more at stake than selecting the right fish for supper.

It had taken no small amount of talking before she had convinced David to allow her to try her plan. She had argued that a woman would be able to ask questions no man would be able to get away with, and that the people of Ziph would never guess a woman had been sent in to find out the news, whereas Abinidab, along with any other man, would be recognized as an emissary from David's camp immediately, putting them all in danger. David had thought it madness, but as she talked, explaining her position, arguing for why it would be safer for all of them, David had become convinced to give it a try. He would send a convoy of men behind her to stand guard from afar.

"My brave Abigail," he'd said, as she put on a clean gown and saddled up a donkey for the ride into Ziph. "Be safe."

"I will send word as soon as I have news," Abigail promised.

In the market, Abigail wandered between tables, touching pomegranates gently, running her fingers over soft linen fabrics. She smiled at a kind-looking older woman in the stall selling cooking pots and said, "These are beautifully made."

"Thank you," the woman said. Her face was lined, and her hair was tucked up under her scarf, but Abigail could see that it was gray around the edges. She looked like the sort of woman who knew what was going on in town. "My husband makes them each by hand. He takes care with each one, and they are all made out of high-quality materials."

"I can see that," Abigail said, touching a pot gently. The metal was hot from the sun, but it was well-crafted. She pretended to examine it carefully. "It is beautifully done."

"Thank you."

Abigail *did* need a new cooking pot. And if she bought one, she thought this woman might be a bit more willing to talk.

"How much are you asking for it?"

The woman named a price, and Abigail bargained her down. They finally agreed on a price, and she handed the pot to Abigail.

"I haven't seen you around here before," the older woman said.

"No, I am new to the area," Abigail said truthfully. "And I am still settling in. But I will admit, I am not sure of the safety of this town. I keep hearing rumors that there is a band of transients staying not too far away. It makes me nervous."

"That would be David and his followers." The woman's distaste for them was obvious in her voice. "Rebels. Trying to overthrow the king or some such nonsense. Do not fear. They will be gone from here soon enough. A group of leaders from town has already sent word to King Saul to let him know their location. His army will be here to chase them away soon enough."

"I am glad to hear it." Abigail tried to act relieved, though on the inside, her heart was beating quickly. "It is terrible to feel unsafe in your own home." She thanked the woman, and then she stopped at a few more stalls, making small purchases, just in case anyone was watching. Then, she hurried to the gates and gave word to the men waiting outside.

"The elders of the town have betrayed us. A delegation has already left for Saul's camp. We must leave right away."

The men thanked her and rode hard back toward camp. They would rouse the camp and get the packing started. By the time Abigail and her servants got back, the camp would be ready to move.

When she returned to camp, they were all waiting for the ram's horn to blow, the signal that it was time to start. Kai and Talia had packed up her tent while she was on her way back. Ahinoam was sitting next to Channah, and when Abigail met her eye, Ahinoam gave her a slight nod.

"Tell me what happened," David said when he saw her. His face was clouded, but she could not tell if he had been worried about her or if he was upset that Saul was still pursuing him. She told him, and he thanked her, perfunctorily, and then he moved to the front of the group and blew the ram's horn. He was concerned, she knew. The weight of this responsibility was heavy on his shoulders. And yet she could not deny that it still stung to be dismissed so quickly, and after what she had just done.

"Come, mistress," Anna said, reaching out to touch her shoulder. "It is time to start moving again." Anna knew her well enough not to say anything about what Abigail was feeling, though Abigail was sure she understood.

As they began to move, David sent out spies to determine exactly where Saul and his men were to see if they were close. When sundown came, they stopped to camp, but David sent out an order that no cooking fires were to be lit to give them away.

That night, Abigail and her servants lay on blankets on the ground, each family clustered together, the scent of fear permeating the darkness. The children were fed bread and some water, and mothers endeavored to keep their little ones quiet. While the younger children were able to fall into exhausted sleep, most of the people slept with one ear listening for any strange sounds, the sound of soldiers. The moon was bright and full, and milky white light bathed the whole area.

Abigail looked up at the stars. If only her father could see her now. Her clothes dirty, sleeping on a blanket outside because they could not make the sound of setting the tent pegs. Men watched over the animals, trying to keep them from making noise.

Abigail heard a stirring, and she squinted through the inky darkness. Some of the men were moving about. Abigail recognized David's dim form, even in the darkness. She heard the sound of swords clanging against the hard ground. She wanted to push herself up, to go see him, to warn him to be careful, but she dared not. She watched, holding her breath, as David and the other men quietly made their way out of camp. Abigail turned over and saw, just a short distance away, Ahinoam also watching the men disappear into the night.

Abigail prayed in the darkness, begging the God Who Saves to preserve and protect the man He had called.

Day broke, and still David and his men had not returned. The people ate a bit of cold bread, and then they broke up the camp and prepared the carts so they would be ready to go when David returned. Word passed through the camp that David had gone to spy out Saul's camp himself.

Just as the dawn was breaking, David and the other two men returned to the camp, whooping and singing. Everyone rushed to see what was happening. Something had certainly changed from when these men had left the camp in the night.

David climbed up on a small rise and addressed the crowd gathered before him. He stood tall and broad against the sunlight, and he was grinning. "We have a reprieve," he said. "Saul has promised not to pursue us."

A cheer went up, and there was much excitement and many hugs. It took some time for the crowd to quiet again so David could explain what had happened.

"We went out in the night to see Saul's camp, and the Lord God was on our side. He caused Saul and his guards to fall into a deep sleep—"

Abishai, one of the warriors who had accompanied David, used his hand to indicate someone drinking from a cup, and they all understood Abishai's suggestion that too much wine might have had something to do with their stupor. David elbowed him and continued on. "The Lord caused them to fall into a deep sleep, and we were able to get right up next to Saul."

"It was the perfect opportunity to run him through with a sword," Abishai said, shaking his head at David. But there was a smile on his face. "We would be able to stop running, and David could be crowned king, as has been promised." A few cheers went up, but Abishai continued, "But David would not do it."

David looked out over the gathered crowd until he found Abigail, and his eyes locked on hers before he said, "It is not my place to kill the Lord's anointed. Either Saul will die in battle or of old age, or even be struck down by the Lord, but it was not my place to kill him."

There was a murmuring among the people. Many appeared to side with Abishai, but Abigail smiled, and felt a warmth spreading throughout her body. David had listened to her words. He had taken her advice.

Joab took up the story. "We took Saul's spear and a jug of water, and we got away without Saul seeing us or anyone even waking up."

Several people laughed, imagining it, and David went on, "We climbed a hill opposite the camp and made sure we were a safe distance away…"

"Then David called out to Saul's general, Abner," Eleazar said. "And he taunted him."

Abishai added, "Then Saul recognized David's voice, and David told him he had Saul's spear and jug of water, that he had been right next to him and yet had spared his life."

David spoke again, growing more animated as the story unfolded. He had the whole camp hanging on each word he said. "I asked him why he was chasing me. To tell me what I have done and what crime he held against me. I told him he has driven me from my home so that I can no longer live among my own people, and I've been told to go worship pagan gods. Am I to die on foreign soil, far from the presence of the Lord?"

There were a few cheers, and several people clapped. David was good at whipping the crowd up.

"And then the most incredible thing happened. This is how we know the Lord God was behind the encounter."

Abigail had known that David was a great warrior, a wonderful musician, and a committed leader. But she hadn't realized until this moment that he was also a great performer. He seemed to know exactly how to speak to the gathered crowd to have them hanging on his every word.

"Friends, Saul confessed that he had sinned and asked me to come back home. He called me his son, and said he would no longer try to harm me because we had valued his life this day."

A collective cry of joy went up among the people, and Abigail wondered if this meant they could truly go home now.

"I told him to let one of his young men come to collect his spear," David continued. "Then Saul gathered his men and left the area. When they were a cloud of dust in the distance I returned to camp to tell you."

The people began to cheer and hug each other. Saul had gone. They would be left alone. Joy filled the camp. David watched them, and as Eleazar and Abishai and Joab went to join their families, he stood quietly in thought. Abigail waited. As soon as the crowd thinned out, she would go to him. But as she stood there, Ahinoam approached David.

"I am glad for your safety, my lord." Her eyes were shining with hope.

David smiled at Ahinoam, but his eyes sought out Abigail's.

She held her breath. It was David's choice. Ahinoam was his wife before Abigail arrived and he'd neglected her lately, preferring his nights with Abigail. But David hesitated and then turned away from Ahinoam, using a finger to summon Abigail.

Abigail stepped forward. She caught the look Ahinoam shot her before she stepped back. Even from here Abigail could see she was fighting to maintain her composure, and there was nothing but hatred in her eyes as she ceded her place to Abigail. What little bit of trust they had built had quickly eroded.

Abigail hated that they had to share the man they loved. But she could not help the flush of excitement and anticipation that rushed through her as she walked toward David. He watched her as she made her way toward him, a smug smile on his face, which only made her heart beat faster.

All around them, people were rushing to set up tents and start cooking fires, and she saw that someone had already set David's tent up. He pulled the flap open and led her inside, and it fell closed behind them. It took a moment for her eyes to adjust to the dim lighting after the brightness of the day, but slowly his form emerged. He led her to the stack of mats in the corner, but when she lay next to him, he did not touch her. Instead, he lay on his back and looked up toward the animal skin above him.

"I am glad you are safe, my lord," she said, reaching out her hand to touch his arm.

He nodded, his hair brushing against the mat beneath them, but did not answer. He did not move her hand away, but he did not respond to her attentions either.

"Were you really just a short distance from King Saul?"

Again David nodded, and then he let out a long breath and turned over to his side. "I could not have gotten so close unless the Lord had granted His favor. And that was when I knew that you were right."

She could not help the smile that spread across her face.

"I knew that the Lord had not granted me this opportunity so that I could shed the blood of His anointed but so that He could show His power more dramatically."

"God is faithful," she said quietly. Her hand was still on his arm, but he did not seem to even notice, and she pulled it back slowly.

"And you are wise." He adjusted the mats under his head and looked at her. "I did not know what a treasure I got when I married you. I saw only how beautiful you were and how you could contribute to the camp."

The words stung, though she knew he did not intend them to. He had wanted her for what she could contribute to the camp. Had Zelek been right that he'd married her for her money?

"But I did not know the Lord was granting me a wise and faithful wife as well," David said. "I am grateful for your advice that I should not hurt the king."

"I am glad," she said. "And now, we do not have to fear Saul at all. We can stay here, or even find a more hospitable place to set up camp."

If they weren't on the run, maybe they could even move out of the tents into more permanent structures. They'd find a place near a stream, and build houses, and she would raise her sons in a settled, stable place.

"Saul will never leave us alone." David rolled onto his back again.

"But—" Abigail did not understand. "You said…"

"I know what I said," David said quietly. He had lost the bravado that had attended his words when he had delivered them to the group. Now he spoke quietly, as if he were haunted. "I reported faithfully the words that came from Saul's mouth. He called me his son and said he will not try to harm me again."

"But you do not believe him." She saw it plainly now.

"I do not think he knows what he says. I believe he has lost his mind. I think he will do anything to maintain his power."

She saw now that David was conflicted. What he had reported to the people with great fanfare and excitement was not a lie, but it was not the whole truth either. Not by far. The man he showed his people, the leader of this great tribe of followers, was not the same as the man he was in private, confused and humbled and searching. She wanted to comfort him, to pull him to herself, to make him forget his worries, even for a few moments, but she could see that what he wanted from her right now was not her body.

"So what will you do?" she asked quietly.

"I do not know." He let out a long breath. "I fear there is nowhere in Israel where we will be safe from the king's rampages. He will come for me again. It's not a question of if; it really is just a question of when."

Abigail thought through his words.

"My lord?"

A pause before he answered, "Yes?"

"You say that you do not know where in Israel we will be safe from King Saul."

"Yes?"

She considered her words one more time before she hurriedly blurted them out. "What if we did not stay in Israel?"

"What do you mean?"

"I mean, Saul can only threaten us if we stay within the boundaries of his kingdom, right?"

David was nodding, following.

"So why don't we leave his kingdom?"

"And go where?" David asked. He was incredulous. "Into the lands of our enemies?"

"Can the Philistines or the Geshurites or the Amalekites or any of the others really be any more dangerous than King Saul and his armies?"

David did not say anything for a moment, and then quietly he said, "It is an interesting idea."

He looked up toward the roof of the tent for a few moments, and then Abigail saw his eyes start to close. His breathing became slow and shallow. She realized he had fallen asleep.

Not long ago, it would have been unthinkable for David to be this close to her without their taking delight in one another's bodies. But already, she could see something between them had changed. The passion she felt for him had not cooled, but his mind was elsewhere.

Which was as it should be, she reminded herself. He was her husband, but he was also the leader of this great group. His mind needed to be focused on keeping them safe.

Abigail rolled onto her side and scooted up close to him, and he draped an arm over her body in his sleep. For the first time in a while, she felt safe. She listened to the sound of his breathing and felt his warmth against her back, and finally she fell into a restful sleep.

CHAPTER FOURTEEN

❖

Early the next morning, David sat outside his tent and began to play his harp. He had composed a song about the confrontation with Saul. Only Abigail knew what the song was really about. She had returned to her tent, but she and Ahinoam, along with the other people of the camp, gathered to listen.

> Have mercy on me, O God, have mercy!
> > I look to you for protection.
> I will hide beneath the shadow of your wings
> > until the danger passes by.
> I cry out to God Most High,
> > to God who will fulfill his purpose for me.
> He will send help from heaven to rescue me,
> > disgracing those who hound me.
> My God will send forth his unfailing love and faithfulness.

Abigail listened to his strong voice ringing out over the camp, and realized it was no wonder his men followed him without question. They saw how dedicated he was to their God and how God had protected them all because of him. Now he told of the traps set for him and how weary he was from distress, yet his heart was trusting in his God. She listened as he continued.

> My heart is confident in you, O God;
>> my heart is confident.
>> No wonder I can sing your praises!
> Wake up, my heart!
>> Wake up, O lyre and harp!
>> I will wake the dawn with my song.
> I will thank you, Lord, among the people.
>> I will sing your praises among the nations.
> For your unfailing love is as high as the heavens.
>> Your faithfulness reaches to the clouds.
> Be exalted, O God, above the highest heavens.
>> May your glory shine over all the earth.

When he had finished and the last notes died away, Abigail felt like she had been in the presence of the Most High. Silence reigned over the camp for a moment and then the people drifted away to various tasks. David bowed his head and then slowly stood up. He turned to one of his men and said, "Gather the leaders and meet me in my tent."

The women went about their duties, but Abigail kept an eye on David's tent. Something was happening. Would they be moving again? But a little while later, David and his men emerged from the tent. David went first to Ahinoam's tent, where he kissed her gently and said something that made her mouth fall open, and then to Abigail's.

"Please pray for our protection on this errand," David said quietly as he leaned in to kiss her.

"Where are you going?"

"It is better you do not know."

Abigail could not help wondering if he had told Ahinoam more.

"But please, pray for us all."

Abigail promised that she would, and then she watched as he strode across the camp and mounted his horse. She saw that they had packed enough food and water to be gone for a lengthy journey. She watched as they rode off, and she did pray. She prayed that God the Protector would go in front of them to clear the way and behind them, and that God would keep His chosen one in the center of His watch.

Life in the camp continued while the men were gone. The unbearable heat of the summer was giving way to cooler days, and their camp's position near a grove of trees allowed for some fresh breezes. Zelek's regular deliveries had necessarily ceased once they had left the Maon Valley, and much of the gold Abigail had brought to the camp had already been spent on provisions for the people, but the supply dwindled further while David and his men were gone. It was no easy task to venture into the nearest town and return with enough grains, lentils, oil, and greens to feed six hundred families without arousing suspicions of why such a great quantity of food was needed, but so far Yahweh had protected them.

Abigail spent the days weaving on her loom, working on a blanket that would keep their baby warm. Abigail had not missed her monthly courses yet, but she felt sure it would happen soon. She spent her nights lying in the tent with her maids, whom she now knew better than ever before. She knew that Kai sometimes talked in her sleep, and that Talia had a summer cold that often kept her up coughing in the night. Abigail became friendly with some of the other women in the camp, including Joab's wife, Raya, who had a big throaty laugh and several young children, and a woman named Shobal, who was quick with a joke and very clever.

One evening, Channah came to her tent and asked for Abigail to come quickly. Abigail followed her to Ahinoam's tent, and inside, she found Ahinoam curled on up a mat in a pool of blood. She was facing the wall, sobbing.

"I don't know what to do," Channah confessed.

Abigail quickly took in the situation. This was not the normal monthly bleeding. This was something else. How had Abigail not noticed she was with child?

"Run back to my tent and ask Anna for the pouch of herbs." A woman in Maon had recommended some herbs to ease the pain of her monthly bleeding, and Abigail hoped that might help now, with the physical pain, at least. She suspected there was another kind of pain gripping Ahinoam that would take far longer to heal. Channah ran off, and Abigail approached the mat cautiously.

"Ahinoam," she said. The woman did not move. Ahinoam had not spoken to her since the night David had chosen her, and she had kept her gaze away. Abigail knew she was probably the last person Ahinoam wanted by her bedside at this moment.

Still, Abigail came forward and sat down next to her and put her hand on her shoulder. She knew Ahinoam realized she was there, but she did not stop her crying. Abigail knew she should find some clean cloths to collect the flow of blood, or at least clean her up, but she dared not. Not yet.

Channah came back with the herbs, and Abigail directed her to mix them with water, and together, they coaxed Ahinoam to sit up and sip. Her eyes were red, and the skin around them was puffy. She had been crying for some time, Abigail could see. Ahinoam did not meet Abigail's eyes.

"I am so sorry," Abigail said. Ahinoam did not acknowledge her. "Please, drink. It will help you feel better."

Ahinoam sipped, and then she gave a sad kind of laugh. "It is your good fortune today, Abigail. You may be the first to give David a child after all."

Abigail shook her head. "No, Ahinoam. It is not my good fortune. It is a terrible thing, and I am sorry for your loss."

Ahinoam shook her head gently.

"I have lost a child too," Abigail said.

Ahinoam turned to her now.

"I was further along than you were. The child was born dead, with the cord wrapped around his neck."

Ahinoam gasped, and Abigail continued. "But it does not matter when the child is lost. My grief is not worse for having been with the child longer. It is a terrible thing, and I would not wish it on anyone."

Ahinoam was looking at her differently now. Something in her look had softened.

"Please, drink. I know it tastes bad, but it will help."

Once Ahinoam had finished the cup of herbs, she allowed Abigail to clean her up and change the bedding. Abigail asked Channah to find some cloths, and she urged Ahinoam to hold them between her legs to help catch the flow of blood. Abigail stayed in the tent through the night and into the next morning, when Ahinoam finally fell into an exhausted sleep.

After that night, a truce of sorts settled between them. They were not friends exactly, but Ahinoam no longer treated Abigail as if she were her enemy. They spoke sometimes, about little things in the camp, and one night Ahinoam even told Abigail about her family, back in Jezreel, and about her three younger sisters whom she missed desperately.

One day, just as they were cleaning up from the evening meal, the hoofbeats of approaching horses sounded. Abigail emerged from her tent and craned her neck to see who approached. There were shouts of excitement from the edge of the camp, and she gathered that these were welcome visitors.

It did not take long for word to spread through the camp that David and his men had returned, and David sent word for the people to gather together. Abigail felt her shoulders unhitch when she saw David standing there, whole and unharmed and even more handsome than ever. He found her in the crowd and met her eye, and she saw in the small smile that curled his lips that he had missed her too. She would soon be able to hold him safe in her arms again.

When all had gathered, David faced his people from the small rise and began to speak. "For the sake of our wives and children, we cannot keep moving in this manner. The king has said he will not seek me, but he has proven himself untrustworthy too many times. He will seek me again, no matter what he has said."

Many of the people seemed confused by this declaration, as the last announcement they had heard was that they were safe from the king's wrath. But there were also many within the crowd who were nodding, believing the truth of his words. Abigail spotted Ahinoam in the crowd, and saw that she was in agreement.

"We have been on a journey to meet with Achish, son of Maoch, King of Gath."

Several people around the gathering let out gasps. She too recognized that name. Gath was a large city in Philistine territory, the capital of the region, and Achish was one of the Philistine rulers.

"Achish has offered us protection from Saul, and he is allowing us to settle in the town of Gath. We will not be on the run any longer. We will settle there, and we will be safe."

Abigail knew she should not be surprised by the news. It was she, after all, who had suggested to David that they might find safety outside of Israel. But it was still shocking to hear that they would be venturing into Gath. The Philistines could not be trusted. They were the sworn enemies of Israel, and wanted nothing more than to wipe their people away and inhabit their lands.

"Why are we going among our enemies?" a voice shouted. "They will kill us!"

David acknowledged the speaker with a nod. "I understand your fear, but Achish has agreed to give us sanctuary. He welcomes us as enemies of Saul."

"The Philistines cannot be trusted!" someone in the crowd shouted. Others echoed the sentiment, and one man yelled out, "They will slaughter us and our families."

The people continued to murmur. It sounded like a hive of bees. Some of the women began to weep, no doubt fearing for their children.

David held up a hand and answered. "I have been assured by Achish that we will be safe. The Philistines will not harm us, and we will be protected from the attacks of King Saul."

Now the murmuring began to quiet down. Abigail knew they trusted David's judgment, for he had kept them safe all this time. They also knew he moved as the Lord led him.

Finally, one voice called out. "We will go where you lead, David."

Others chimed in. "We will go."

Then the entire camp answered with one voice. They would go.

David took a breath, looked out over the crowd, and said, "Yahweh will protect us, as He always has. We leave at first light."

He turned and stepped off the rise, and there was much confusion in the moments that followed. Though they said they trusted him, many felt that David had lost his mind, that he was leading them to their deaths. Abigail watched the reaction, fear settling in her belly. Could they trust King Achish? The Philistines were fierce warriors, conquerors who wanted to inhabit the land God had promised to Israel. They were savages. They killed children for sport, she'd heard, and practiced all kinds of evil good people could not even begin to imagine. All her life, she had feared them more than any other threat. And now they were going to seek protection among them? Abigail held her breath. Had she been the cause of this madness?

David strode through the crowd toward Abigail, and when he reached her, he pulled her in for a long, deep kiss. But that night, he did not call for her, and in the morning, when she saw Ahinoam emerge from David's tent, Abigail could not bring herself to hate her.

CHAPTER FIFTEEN

The next morning, David's six hundred men, their wives, children, and all their belongings began the arduous trip from the mountains of Israel to Gath, the capital of Philistia. The journey took five days, since they were forced to move at the pace of the animals and children. For once they were not moving to another temporary camp, but to someplace they could stay for some length of time. Abigail's mind turned as she walked. How long would they be able to stay in the land of the Philistines? She knew David was a prize that some wanted to capture, yet the king Achish had given his word that they could have sanctuary in Gath. How trustworthy was this king?

As the people approached the ancient city built on a hill, Abigail stared at the massive iron gates. They were built to keep the enemy out—or perhaps keep people in? The city had thick walls all around and looked impregnable. The gates swung open with a great grinding of gears. Achish and some of his soldiers were waiting for them inside the city gates. The smell of burning metal hung in the air. A high-pitched pounding sound rang out at irregular intervals.

The king was sitting on a large throne on a platform in a large open gathering space just beyond the gates. David dismounted and bowed low before the king. "We are most happy to accept the gracious hospitality of your majesty the king. We are grateful for asylum from the king of Israel. We are your servants."

The bedraggled group silently entered the city, the only sounds coming from small children and the animals. They were looking all around, some appraising the enormity of the city, with its golden stone walls that stretched up toward the sky, others stepping forward in fear. Abigail saw it on their faces. No one spoke, for they had agreed David would speak for all of them.

The king smiled, but there was something in it that Abigail didn't trust. Had David been wrong to trust this man? "Welcome. We have prepared housing for all of you."

He gestured to the men with him, and slowly David's entourage was separated by families and shown where they were to lodge. Some families were to share quarters, but none complained, for they were being shown to stone homes. The women delighted in the novelty of real houses with solid walls, and the children shrieked as they explored their new play areas. Achish directed others of his men to show those driving the herds where to keep their animals. The king almost had to shout to be heard over the bleating of the confused sheep and goats.

The king gestured to a large area nearby. "This will be for your horses. Feed has been provided for you."

The men and their families carted belongings, crying babies, and small children to their different locations. Abigail wanted to put a scarf over her nose to try to block out the smell of burning metal, but felt it might be an insult to the king.

Abigail and Ahinoam were summoned forward, and David introduced them to the king. Abigail bowed low before him, and when she straightened she saw that he was eyeing her appreciatively. He glanced at David, cocking an eyebrow, and then back at her, nodding. Abigail pretended not to notice and she studied the king, a swarthy man with a broad chest. He was not tall, but solidly built. Dark, bushy eyebrows accented eyes that seemed to dart everywhere, taking in the scene before him. He seemed friendly enough, but it took more willpower than she had to overcome a lifetime of fear. David trusted this man, so she tried to as well. She watched David's people cast surreptitious glances at their benefactor. They could only count on the fact that they trusted David implicitly, and not a murmur was heard about the move to Philistine territory.

David was given his own quarters, while Abigail and Ahinoam and their maidservants followed one of the soldiers. He scowled at them and said no more than necessary as he took them to one of the larger houses. They would share it together. Each eyed the other nervously. Now they would both be aware of when the other came and went from David's quarters. A delicate sense of truce had settled between them, but would this new arrangement upset that?

Abigail appraised the house assigned to them. It was built of yellowish stone, quarried locally, judging by the color of the hills that surrounded them. There were three rooms arranged around a courtyard on the first floor, and two rooms upstairs. The kitchen was off the main house but connected by a passageway. It was a large house, and well arranged, but it was covered in dust. It was obvious no one had lived here for some time. Was it because of the smell of metal in the air? The smelter was not far away, it appeared.

Abigail nodded to Ahinoam. "We have work to do." She set her maidservants to work to clean their new quarters from top to bottom. Anna, Talia, Kai, and Yelena had been relatively quiet during the entrance into the city, but now they had something familiar to do. Anna set about arranging Abigail's personal things, setting up her loom carefully in the corner of her chamber, while Channah did the same for Ahinoam, and then they began to help with the cleaning. Anna wielded the handmade broom they carried with them from camp to camp, as the other women got out cloths to begin the dusting.

As Abigail worked, she thought back to the moment she and Ahinoam turned from the king's presence to follow the soldier to their quarters. She had overheard an exchange between David and the king.

"When you are settled, come to me and we will discuss your duties," Achish had said.

David had bowed again to the king. "As you wish, my king."

Abigail could not help but wonder what the king meant. What had David promised in exchange for their safety?

CHAPTER SIXTEEN

Abigail and her household settled in to their new life in Gath. David and the men often vanished during the day, coming home tired and sore and bloodied, and Abigail, like most of the women she knew, chose not to ask too many questions. They had finally reached a state of tenuous security, and as long as David continued to seek the Lord's guidance, who were they to argue? Abigail had also reached a certain amount of accord with Ahinoam. She shed some tears on the nights David called for Ahinoam, but during the day they had settled into a certain kind of uneasy companionship.

One night, many weeks after they had arrived, Abigail stood with David on the rooftop of his quarters looking up at the stars. He had called her to his bed, but their time together was over quickly. His body was there with her, but his mind was elsewhere. Afterward, though, he led her out onto the roof of his house, which was positioned on a rise, from which they could survey the whole city. He talked to her about his dreams for the future, what kind of palace he wanted to build and where he would set up the Ark of the Covenant. He had learned many new techniques from the Philistines, including the forging of iron, that would allow for the construction of structures like their people had never seen. After he described the soaring roof and the heated tubs he wanted to build, he went quiet, lost in thought.

"You had a messenger yesterday," she said after a few moments. "Was it good news?"

"It was a note from Jonathan, the king's son." David was leaning against the low wall, looking out over the houses where his people were arrayed. The moon was waning, but the fires from the smelter on the edge of town meant it never really grew fully dark here. "He sent a letter to me secretly by a trusted courier."

"What does he say?" David had told her, in the long, leisurely days of their first week together, about his friendship with Jonathan. He was the one who had first warned David that Saul was plotting to kill him and urged him to flee the palace. She wondered about Jonathan's sister Michal, David's first wife, but could not bring herself to ask.

"He grows ever more concerned about his father. He says he grows madder by the day and is so consumed with trying to find me that he neglects many of his duties."

"I am sorry to hear it." Abigail stood next to David. She liked to see which of the houses still had cooking fires burning and guess what the people inside were doing. "He still fears you, even now when you are so far from Gibeah?"

"He fears that now we have settled here, we have aligned ourselves with the Philistines and will fight with them against the armies of Israel."

"But we would not do that."

David did not say anything. An uneasy sense of dread spread through her.

"You would lead our people to fight against the Lord's people?" she asked.

His face was silhouetted in the moonlight. He was still as handsome as ever, but his brow was furrowed and the strain of the past few months was showing in the area around his eyes. He seemed to be considering his response. When he did speak, it came out as a sigh. "I do not know."

"What do you mean you do not know?"

A year ago, Abigail would not have been able to imagine speaking to any man in this way. Certainly not her husband, to say nothing of the man who would be king. Women did not question their husbands; they existed to serve them. She could never have spoken to Nabal this frankly, or her father, or any man in her life. And yet David had always been different. He seemed to encourage her to speak freely, to ask questions, to probe his motives. He seemed to value her thoughts and weigh them as he would weigh the thoughts of a trusted man.

"We have sought refuge in the land of the Philistines," Abigail continued. "That does not mean we are aligned with them. They are the sworn enemies of Israel, the people of Yahweh."

If David had forgotten this, she did not know what she would do.

"We are not aligned with the Philistines," David said. The words came out slowly, like he had to think through each one carefully. "We will continue to serve the one true God, and to wait for the time He sees fit to fulfill His promises."

Yahweh's promise to crown David king being first and foremost, Abigail thought. She nodded.

"But...it is difficult," David said.

"How is it difficult?" She thought back to the snatch of conversation she'd overheard between King Achish and David on the day they'd settled in this town. "What price has the king asked you to pay in exchange for your protection?"

Again, David remained quiet for a moment, surveying the city. She could not guess what was going on in his head.

Finally, he spoke. "King Achish expects that we will fight with him against the Israelites," David said. "If the Philistine army goes into battle, Achish expects that we will join him in the effort."

It was unthinkable. They would be fighting against their own people, and against their God. The God who had brought them out of Egypt and called them His own.

"How did he come to that understanding?" Abigail asked, choosing her words carefully. David was sensitive to anything he believed to be criticism. If she pressed too hard, if she came out and accused him of being dishonest, he would stop talking with her about this.

"I pray daily that it will not come to that," David said. He had not really answered her question. "That Yahweh will rescue us from this situation before it arises."

He was walking a delicate line, she knew. He was waiting for Saul to be removed as king, but he would not kill him himself. And in the meantime they were all at risk.

"And what of the raids Achish sends you on in the meantime?" Abigail asked.

"We do not—"

"Do not lie to me."

David had always appreciated her bravery, he'd said. Now was not the time to allow him to get away with untruths.

David considered, and then seemed to come to a decision. "We do not think of them as raids."

"What do you consider them, then?"

"Tasks required of us."

Abigail thought about the blood that ran through the streets of the city as the men rinsed off their bodies and their clothing when they came home. These were no mere tasks. "And what do these tasks entail?"

"Achish needs supplies." He said it quietly, and she could tell he was not proud of his words.

"So you go into a city and take these supplies and return to him with the spoils."

David nodded. There was a lot he was not saying, she knew. He already told her much more than most would say he should.

"And these cities, these tasks." A breeze brought the smell of burning metal through the air. "These are Israelite settlements that you…visit?"

"No." David said it almost like a confession. "Achish thinks we are entering border settlements on the Israelite side, but I could not do that. I cannot take from our own people."

"So you are entering Philistine cities and taking…supplies… from them, but Achish believes you are stealing from the Israelites."

David nodded. It was a dangerous game he was playing. He was risking all their lives, playing tricks on the Philistine king. "It is the Geshurites, the Girzites, and the Amalekites."

"And what of the people in those cities? Are you not worried they will get word back to Achish about what you have done?"

"We leave no one behind to bring word to him," David said simply.

Abigail took in that news, turning it over in her mind. She had known it on some level, but it was still shocking to hear it said outright. David was a warrior, celebrated for killing tens of thousands. It was what had made him so valuable to Saul, and what made him so fearful for Saul now. She had known all of this about him when she had married him. And yet she hadn't seen then how it weighed on him. How the ways of war were a burden, and yet he did not take his duties lightly.

"The Lord has given us our homeland," David said. "And He has promised that all the tribes of Israel will be united in it."

"But isn't there another way?" Abigail asked. "Is not every life precious to our God?"

"Every life is important," David agreed. "Every person has God's breath in their bodies. But God's plan is bigger than ours. He has called us all to make sacrifices for His kingdom. I cannot question what He has called me to do. I can only act in faithfulness." He rested his palms on the wall and gazed out over the city.

"Does faithfulness have to involve so much bloodshed?"

David shrugged. "I dare not question Yahweh. He has shown many times through our history that there is no deliverance without bloodshed."

Abigail knew the Law of Moses, and she knew that blood sacrifice was required as atonement for sin. And Abigail remembered the blood her people had spread on their doorways and the horror that had literally passed over them while the Egyptian mothers mourned. She nodded. She did not understand it, but Yahweh's ways were not their ways.

And yet she wished there were another way. A better way. For all David's noble talk of sacrifice, it did not quite ring true. Was slaughtering a city of people truly sacrifice? For what was sacrifice if it did not cost you anything? Was it really sacrifice if it was not something precious to you that you were giving up?

It was blasphemy to question Yahweh—to even think it—but she could not help but wonder why He didn't give up something precious to Himself if He truly wanted to save His people.

"Is every sacrifice worth making?" Abigail asked.

David did not answer her for some time, just looked out over the city. Finally, he spoke. "What else can we do?"

Abigail thought for a moment. She did not have an answer to the larger question, that of deliverance and redemption. But she did have an idea for how their people might gain a measure of safety.

"If we move away from Gath, you will not see Achish so much," Abigail said. "And there will be less chance he will hear where you are actually going on your raids."

David nodded.

"Could you ask the king for another place to settle?"

David turned his face toward her and gazed at her, and then he stepped closer. For just a brief moment, she thought he was looking at her the way he had in the earliest days of their marriage, when he couldn't seem to stop looking at her and couldn't make himself stop touching her. But then, instead of taking her into his arms, he said to her, "How did you get to be so wise? I have come to value your opinions highly."

She knew it was high praise. She knew she should be thrilled to be so valued by a man such as David. But as they stood there on that rooftop, the stars spread out in the endless sky above them, all she felt was disappointment.

◆

The next morning, when he slipped out of her arms and dressed, she rolled over and watched him. He strapped on his sword and his breastplate. They would be going on another raid today, then.

"Be safe, my lord," she said.

David leaned over and brushed his lips across her forehead. "I will trust in the leading of the Lord our God. He has protected us so far."

"You are the future king of Israel. Surely He will protect you until you come into your anointed destiny."

He raised an eyebrow. "I am counting on that," he murmured quietly, and strode out of the tent to meet his men.

In the silence that was left behind, Abigail prayed that Yahweh would protect David, but she also prayed that He would give her husband wisdom to lead his people well. She guessed there was much more than she'd yet understood at stake.

CHAPTER SEVENTEEN

It was less than a week later that David called a meeting of his people in the gathering place near the city gates.

"King Achish has been so pleased with our work here in Gath that he has offered us a more comfortable home in the town of Ziklag," David called out. There were murmurs and a few gasps of excitement. Ziklag was a country town, surrounded by fields. It would be less busy and less foul-smelling than here in Gath.

One of his men spoke up. "You have led us wisely so far. This is a good move. There will be closer pasturelands for our sheep."

Several others voiced their agreement. Only Abigail wondered what David had really said to the king to get him to let them go to the rural town. Surely he did not want David and his people out of his grasp, not now. However, she was relieved. This would mean that there was less of a chance that his true movements would be revealed to the king.

Soon their part of the town rang with voices as the people once again packed their belongings and prepared to move. The town of Ziklag was over twenty miles away. With children and animals, it would take at least three days to reach the town. David's people were seasoned travelers by now and were ready to move out in short order. Clothing, kneading troughs, and cooking gear had once again been collected and packed on the donkeys as the company prepared to move out of Gath. All the provisions they could gather were packed, along with wine and plenty of water. They did not know the lay of the land or what streams were available.

The king came to bid them farewell and promised a visit in the near future. Abigail knew that David agreed to continue to supply the king with goods from his raids.

Glad to finally be free of the smell of burning metal, Abigail walked steadily with the other women. Small children rode in what carts were available. Others rode on horseback with their fathers or other men who volunteered, while mothers carried their babies in slings on their backs.

She took in the fresh air of the fields again and relished the day that was hot but not stifling. She walked most of the time, since her maids also had to walk. When she showed signs of weariness, they insisted she ride her donkey. David rode back and forth along the line of people, encouraging them.

At sundown, they set up camp, and the land was dotted with cooking fires. There was the sound of children and adult voices. Someone played a flute, and it sounded a happy note in the evening stillness. The air was filled with the smell of lentil stews and other meals that could be cooked quickly. When the camp settled down for the night, Abigail, Ahinoam, and their servants could get needed rest, knowing David had assigned watchmen throughout the night all around the camp.

Abigail lay on her pallet and looked up at the stars. She marveled at the seemingly endless number of them. More than she could count. It was a reminder to her that their God watched over them, always. A night bird called in the distance, and she closed her eyes. They would be up at dawn, on the move again.

Two days later, as they neared the town of Ziklag, good grazing land came into view. Those who tended the small flocks of sheep and goats turned the animals toward the vast meadows.

As they entered the town, residents eyed them curiously. The Israelites filled the narrow streets, walking two and three across. Abigail noted that there were wells in the town that would provide an ample water supply. Many of David's people had been hungry for the vegetables and fruits they had known in Israel. There were signs of many crops and fruit trees here.

The countryside was flat. It would allow David's lookouts to observe the land in all directions from the top of the wall, so no enemy could sneak up on them. The walls of Ziklag would provide safety for their people.

Once again, following the directions of the king, the people were distributed around the town to homes that were available. As before, Abigail, Ahinoam, and the five maidservants occupied a house together, and families had to share their quarters. No one complained, for they felt they at least had a respite, not only from Gath and the smelter, but also from constant moving around the country. Many had felt vulnerable in the Philistine capital and were relieved to be so far away.

When they were settled, David sent for Abigail many times, far more times than he sent for Ahinoam, but as time went by, there was still no sign of a child. On the times she watched Ahinoam leave for David's quarters, Abigail wrestled with jealousy. It was hard to bear any other woman in David's arms. She had to remind herself Ahinoam was his wife before her. She bowed her head in remorse, repenting of her thoughts. It was the way things were, and she had come willingly. She turned to her loom, where she spent much time working beautiful and delicate fabrics.

For a year and four months, David and his people lived quietly in Ziklag among the Philistines. Late at night as they lay in his bed, David told Abigail that the king was delighted with David's prowess and the vast amounts of spoil, sure that the Israelites now hated David for raiding their towns. Abigail wondered how much longer he could keep up the pretense without the king finding out. Surely somewhere along the line someone would escape from one of David's raids and get a message to the king. Abigail shuddered to contemplate the consequences.

One day, as they were sitting down for a meal, Abigail noticed a swelling in Ahinoam's belly. She looked again, and saw that her bosom was larger, and her eyes were shining, her skin seeming to glow.

How had Abigail not noticed before? How could she have not seen? Abigail felt a small flame of jealousy tightening her chest. Ahinoam was with child?

"Why did you not tell me?" Abigail asked.

Ahinoam looked down, but there was a smile on her face. "I did not want to upset you."

"I am not upset," Abigail said, and tried her best to make the words true in her heart. "The Lord God has blessed you. You will bear David a child." It took everything in Abigail to say the next part. "May it be his firstborn son."

"I had worried you would be mad," Ahinoam said. "And things have been so much better between us, so I thought…" She did not seem to know how to finish the sentence.

"I am pleased for you," Abigail said. It was true; of course, she would have loved to have borne David's first child, but she was pleased for Ahinoam, whom she had developed tender feelings for in the past year. "May the Lord bless you, and David as well."

But would He ever bless Abigail?

CHAPTER EIGHTEEN

❖

Abigail was at her loom when David returned to Ziklag after his latest trip to Gath to present the spoils of his last raid. He was gone for many days because of the distance of the raids and also the distance to Gath.

But when he returned, he was agitated. Abigail touched him in the night, and he jumped, scared. His mood went from sour to worse at the slightest provocation. He did not speak to anyone, even Abigail. She had not realized how much she had come to appreciate their talks until he would not open up to her. Some of the men that had ridden with him were stoic, silent, and went about their duties with grim faces. Something had happened, and no one would say what it was. The people waited, sensing danger of some kind, but unsure of the source.

Tonight, David had gone to his quarters and closed the door. Abigail knew he must desperately need the Lord's guidance. When alone, he would prostrate himself on the floor before his God.

A sinking sense of dread came over Abigail. Perhaps the king had found out where David had been raiding. There would be retribution. But then, if that had happened, the king's soldiers would have already been there arresting them all, or worse.

It had been many weeks since David had sent for Abigail, but when he did this night, she felt a sense of trepidation. His mind would be elsewhere, and she already knew he would not lavish the attention on her she craved. But she washed with the water from the basin and rubbed scented oil in her hair and put on a clean robe. Eleazar led her into his chamber, where David sat at a small table, hunched over what appeared to be a series of hand-drawn maps. He looked up when she entered, but his smile didn't reach his eyes. She saw there were dark crescents under his eyes, and he appeared to be exhausted.

"My lord," she said as Eleazar walked out and closed the door.

"Abigail." He gestured for her to sit on the wooden chair opposite him. "I am glad you have come."

She did not have a choice, but she did not say that. "What is wrong?"

He leaned back in his chair and eyed her, and this time the small smile appeared to be genuine. "You always do know how to get straight to the point."

"You are not well, my lord. We can all see that something is troubling you. Please tell me how I can be of service." She edged her chair a bit closer to his.

"The Philistines have gone to war against the Israelites," David said, his voice solemn.

Abigail understood exactly what this meant. "And our men must now fight with the Philistines against Israel."

David nodded. "Achish has summoned us to Aphek to join him and the armies of the other four Philistine kings by week's end."

It was unthinkable. They could not march against the Israelites. These were their own people, Yahweh's people. They could not do this.

"You worried this would happen," she said softly.

"It was always a danger of seeking protection in Philistine lands," David said. "It seemed like a risk worth taking to be safe from Saul's armies. But now..." He let his voice trail off.

Abigail wasn't sure what was expected of her in this moment. She sensed she was not here to provide the momentary distraction of taking him to bed, but she did not know what he wanted from her if not her body.

"What do your advisors say?" He met regularly with a group of men, godly and trusted.

"Some say that we should refuse to go. But if we do that, Achish will have us all killed."

She nodded, encouraging him to go on.

"Some say we should go to the battle and secretly fight for Israel."

"Do you think Achish and the other Philistine kings would not notice?"

"It would be a death sentence for sure." He shook his head. "Joab suggests that we fight alongside the Philistines and that any men from Saul's army lost by our swords would be a message to Saul."

There were three bad options, Abigail saw now. It was no wonder David was upset.

"You have sought the Lord's wisdom," Abigail said. "What does He say?"

"I have not heard an answer," David said. "I do not know what He wishes me to do." He rubbed his hand across his chin, and then he looked up, and when he spoke again, his voice was quiet. "Has the Lord abandoned me?"

Abigail had never heard the future king sound so vulnerable. But she was grateful that she knew exactly how to answer.

"The God of Abraham and Moses would not abandon His chosen," she said. "Just because you do not hear Him does not mean He is not there."

"But how am I to know what He wants of me?" David asked. "I believe He hears me, yet He does not answer. How can I act without knowing His will?"

Abigail sat still a moment, trying to choose her words carefully. Had a man ever consulted a woman on such matters? She knew even in that moment how blessed she was that her husband valued her thoughts.

"It is not a small thing I am facing," David continued. "Many lives are at stake. If I choose the wrong course, the future of God's people may be ruined." And then he continued more softly, "Why won't He tell me what He wants from me?"

Abigail did not know. She could not pretend to understand the mind of God. She had no idea what He would want from David in this situation. But she did know His character and that He would always fulfill the promises He made. *Please give me the right words, God of Israel.*

"Perhaps all He wants is for you to trust Him."

David absorbed the words, but the pained look on his face did not change. "I do trust Him. But I do not know what to *do*."

Abigail thought back to the stories she had heard throughout her childhood, which had been passed down through the generations.

"Moses could not see a path forward when he led the Israelites to the edge of the Red Sea," she said quietly. "But the Lord opened a path no one could have expected."

"They walked through the sea on dry land," David said quietly.

"And when there was no food for them? Nothing to eat in the wilderness? Moses could not see how they would survive, and yet God provided manna."

David was nodding, still looking down at the table.

"And do not forget Abraham. He did not know how God would save his son, but he walked in obedience anyway. And at the last moment, God provided a ram."

"You are saying that God will provide a way," David said quietly.

"I do not know what He will do," she said. "And I do not know which path to tell you to take," she said. "But I do know that Yahweh has called you, and if you are seeking to serve Him, He will send deliverance."

David nodded, moving his head slowly, but his eyes were far away.

She reached out and took his hand, and he let her hold it but did not show any other sign that he recalled she was in the room. She sat with him in silence for a while, and then he sent her back to her quarters so he could spend more time talking to God.

Abigail climbed into her own bed, mystified by the turns that her life had taken. Who was she, that David should seek her guidance? She only hoped that the Lord would direct and guide his path.

❖

The next morning, David gathered his people in the square. His face was grave. Abigail was sure he had not slept the previous night.

"My friends, we have enjoyed the hospitality of King Achish for many months now, and so far all has gone well. Now we face a situation that is serious, and I've sought the Lord's wisdom as to what to do."

Some of the people began to murmur among themselves. What could it be? Would they be moving again? Many had puzzled looks on their faces. The women waited silently, stoically, for the news.

"All five kings of the Philistines have decided to go to war again with Israel and King Saul." He took a deep breath. "I and my warriors are expected to join King Achish and the men of Ziklag and march with him into battle."

There was a stunned silence, and then everyone began talking at once.

"Join the king in battle? Against our own people?"

"What are we to do?"

Fear was almost palpable in the assembly. Abigail held her breath, wondering how David was going to proceed.

"We cannot go to war against our own people." Eleazar, one of David's most trusted warriors, stepped forward.

"I agree. But we cannot tell Achish no. It would be suicide to betray him now."

There were murmurs of unbelief like waves throughout the crowd.

David put up a hand. "I have prayed, and I believe our God is going to make a way for us, just as He made a way for Moses to cross the Red Sea, just as He provided a ram for Abraham. Let us pretend to prepare for battle, but each man seek God for wisdom. Deliverance shall come."

Her words sounded more certain when they came from his mouth, but still, Abigail felt herself begin to tremble. Yahweh had protected them many times before, but she could not see how He could possibly work this out now.

There was a stunned silence, and David motioned to Ishbaal, Eleazar, Shammah, and Joab to follow him into his tent. Those in the crowd looked at one another, faces stricken. Slowly, conversations broke out, and eventually everyone began to wander off toward their own homes. From the bits Abigail overhead, she gathered that the people were starting to believe David was as mad as Saul.

The following morning, David and his men prepared for battle. The entire camp was restless, not knowing the outcome of what they considered David's folly.

David called Ahinoam and Abigail to him. "You must be strong for the other women and children. I believe our God has an answer, but we must move forward to obey the king. Deliverance will come for us in God's timing."

He embraced Ahinoam for a few moments and then pulled back and let his hand rest on her rounded belly. Ahinoam looked at him with naked love in her eyes.

"Come back in time to meet your son," Ahinoam said. It was an intimate moment, and Abigail felt bad observing it, but she couldn't make herself look away, no matter how much it twisted at her heart. David nodded, and then he kissed Ahinoam and sent her back to their house. When she was gone, he gestured for Abigail to step forward.

"Please look out for her. You are the strong one," David said. He put an arm around Abigail and drew her to him, kissing her on the top of her head. "The rest will look to you for leadership. The countryside is peaceful, so you should all be safe. We will return as soon as we are able."

"I pray it is so, my lord."

He leaned down and kissed her. He pulled her close, pressing her against him, kissing her hungrily, and for a moment, she thought he would be delaying his journey, but then he remembered himself and pulled away. "I will return soon."

She watched him walk out to the city gates to meet his men, his sword clinking against the ground as he went down the steps. As she walked slowly to her quarters, she could only trust in David's judgment and the will of the Most High.

Abigail stood with the other women and children as the warriors gathered to move out. They watched the men follow

David out of the city and waited until they were only a small cloud of dust on the horizon.

She looked upward.

He is Your anointed, oh Lord. Bring him safely back to me.

She turned away, unable to shake the feeling of apprehension that again swept over her spirit. They were in Yahweh's hands. All she could do was pray.

CHAPTER NINETEEN

❖

The town was peaceful for several days, and the women went about their usual tasks, taking care of their homes and children. But on the fourth day, Anna returned from the well and came to Abigail.

"Mistress, there is a rumor that men have been sighted in the distance."

"Who is it?"

"Perhaps David and his men are returning," Anna said. "Perhaps the Lord has provided a way for them to return safely, just as David said."

Abigail bit her lip. She did not want to alarm Anna, but she knew it would take several days for David and his men to reach the assembly point designated by the king. Even if they were sent home by the Lord's provision as soon as they arrived, it would take several more days for them to return to Ziklag. It was too soon. The men in the distance were not David's. The only men left in town were the old and infirm. They would be no help against an invasion. Abigail knew the gates of the city remained closed. But would they stay that way?

Abigail, Ahinoam, and their maids slept lightly, each woman listening for any sound that disturbed the sleeping city.

The next morning, just as the sun was rising in the east, shouting and screaming awakened Abigail. She rose, and a jolt of fear struck her heart. She did not know what was happening, but she knew she needed to try to get away.

"Come quickly," she commanded her maids, and then she went in to wake Ahinoam. She found the woman trembling, her hand on her stomach, her eyes wide. "Dress and let's go. We must hurry."

She heard the sound of splintering wood and metal upon metal amidst the screams. Who was invading the city, and what did they want? She quickly directed her maids to gather what food they could and hide it under their clothing. She and Ahinoam dressed quickly and put on cloaks. Abigail grabbed what few pieces of jewelry she had brought with her and hid them in her clothing. Just as they were preparing to leave, the door burst open.

Several warriors surveyed the women. "Come with us now," the largest one said. When they did not move immediately, he said, "Do as we say or you will be dead!"

The men grabbed them by the arms and pulled them out of the house. Some of the men took anything in the house they considered valuable as they left while others set fire to the house with torches. Pushed from behind, the women stumbled out into the square to join the other people of the town who had been gathered in a group, their eyes wide with fear. The way they raiders spoke made Abigail think they were Amalekites, but she could not be sure.

They stood quietly, some of the women weeping softly and holding their children to them as they watched the raiders come with armloads of booty to pile nearby. As the men left a building, they set it on fire, and the smoke filled the air. Children began to cry and their mothers quickly shushed them, not wanting to antagonize their captors.

Abigail looked around slowly. A group of men from Ziklag were on the ground tied with ropes. They were old and some were the sick David had left behind. It did not look like anyone had been killed, but these invaders were fierce warriors and showed little pity.

Abigail thought about the raids David and his men went on. Was this what they did? Was this how the people felt? Was he surrounded by mothers trying to protect their children, and showing no mercy? She felt sick imagining it. David only attacked their enemies, she reminded herself, but it did not help much. The Amalekites were enemies of the Israelites.

The leader strutted in front of them. "So your men left you here, a helpless group of old men, women, and children? Did they count on your walls to protect you? How convenient of them to leave all this for us." His eyes raked over Abigail from head to toe. "You will bring a fine price from the slave traders."

Her heart went cold within her. Slave traders? Why had David insisted on riding out to meet with the Philistine army? How could he and the other men leave them so vulnerable? It might be days before David returned—if they ever returned at all—and knew of their plight, and by then it would be too late.

The men tied ropes around their waists, and the women were led stumbling out of the ruined town and forced to walk behind some of the Amalekite raiders. Another group rode behind them to make sure no one escaped.

Abigail looked back at the burning town. It was all David and the men would find when they finally returned.

Abigail thought about what to do. David had been impressed by her bravery, all those years ago. Could she risk a daring rescue now? She looked around but did not see how. She was tied to the other women. Anyone who tried to escape would be killed, and likely the others around her too. There was no place to run.

"It will be all right," she said to Ahinoam, who was cradling her belly, tears running freely down her cheeks.

They walked along, kicking up dust, listening to the constant bleating of sheep and goats as all the animals had been rounded up by the raiders. Many of the men had bags of plunder tied to their saddles and shouted to each other, obviously excited about what they had stolen from the town. Once again, she thought about what David and his men had been doing to Philistine towns, and her stomach turned. David had convinced himself that he was doing God's will. But how could something like this be Yahweh's plan?

Abigail counted over a hundred camels among the raiders, and she gazed wearily at the large, lumbering beasts. She had not seen many camels in her lifetime, except for a caravan that had passed near her home in Maon once. The camels were attended to by Egyptian slaves who served the Amalekites, even on this mission.

Anger rose up within her. Their captors could easily carry some of the children who were tired from their long forced walk, and the women with child, like Ahinoam. As if reading her thoughts, one of the men looked down on her from his camel and sneered as he continued past.

Abigail encouraged her maids and Ahinoam to stick as close to her as they could. Maybe they could all draw strength from each other. Abigail swallowed the fear that threatened to overwhelm her and strove to maintain her courage. It was all she could do for them.

When the group paused for a short rest, women were able to nurse their babies. Some of the warriors stood around and nudged one another, making comments. Abigail was glad she didn't know what they were saying, but she had a good idea. She was glad for once that she had no child that could be taken away by its captors and sold. Some of the raiders looked the women over with lust in their eyes, and Abigail feared for what might come. She could only pray for David to get word, but no one had been left behind to take the message, so how could he hear? He would only know when he and his men returned to Ziklag and found the burned-out town.

Abigail did not understand the Amalekite tongue, but she remembered that the leader had spoken to them in Hebrew. She wondered if she could reason with him in some way. Just then he came by and singled her out as they prepared to march again. He grabbed her by the hair and ran a rough hand over her body. "Perhaps I will keep you for myself," he murmured. "You shall give me sons."

Abigail remained silent, fearing that any words of defiance might cause him to harm her or worse. Ahinoam watched with fear in her eyes, and some of the women sobbed softly. Their faces were dirty from the dust and the children who could walk were getting tired. Women picked up any small children who seemed to lag and carried them.

They were driven for what seemed like hours and finally came to the brook Behor. The water was cold and waist-high, and the women had to hold their small children and babies above the water. None of their captors offered to help. Abigail and the others were thirsty and scooped water into their mouths with one hand and gave water to the children.

Abigail picked up a small boy who was crying for his mother. "Hush, hush, your Imma is nearby. I will keep you safe." She held him close and waded into the water, shivering with the cold. When she reached the other side, her tunic was soaked and her sandals squished as she walked. She had given her cloak to a young woman with a baby and the food she had hidden to another young mother and her children. The Amalekites pushed on, obviously eager to get to a place far from Ziklag.

There was a sudden cry from Kai, and Abigail turned to see Yelena and Talia helping her up from the ground. Kai's foot was bleeding.

"What happened?"

"She stumbled over a rock and cut her foot," Yelena murmured, glancing at the nearby warriors fearfully.

Abigail thought quickly. "Bind it with your sash as quickly as you can."

Yelena tore off her sash and bound the foot. Abigail could only hope they would be given water soon so they could wash the wound. She had seen what happened to wounds that were not cleaned well, but at the moment there was nothing else she could do.

One of their captors spotted them and waved his spear in the air, indicating that they were to keep moving.

Yelena and Talia put their arms around Kai and supported her the best they could. Kai hobbled along, trying her best to keep going.

When they were finally allowed to rest again, Abigail checked on Ahinoam. She said she was feeling all right, but her face showed strain. When their captors tossed them some bread and fruit along with a few leather water bags, Abigail gave Ahinoam her portion.

After the meal, when their guards were occupied talking with each other and the slaves were cleaning up, Abigail quickly unwrapped Kai's wound. It was an ugly, deep cut. There was no way to sew it up. She used as little water as she dared and washed it as well as she could. Tears ran down Kai's cheeks from the pain, but she wept quietly so as not to draw attention to them.

Abigail felt badly for her, but she was worried about more than the pain. If she were wounded, she would be considered damaged by slave traders and they could kill her rather than bother with her wound. Ahinoam also sensed the danger. "We must conceal her as much as possible."

Abigail turned to Kai. "Try to walk as normally as possible. We can only hope it will heal."

Many of the women were helping others, so the two women supporting Kai were glanced at but the guards didn't stop them.

As they passed a field, Abigail saw a young man lying along the road. He was obviously very ill. He looked Egyptian, and she realized his master farther ahead in the caravan had abandoned him there to die. As his eyes met hers, she could only give him a sympathetic look before they were herded on past. In her mind Abigail raged against the Amalekites, abandoning a servant just because he was sick. They were animals.

◆

They had been traveling two days and slept on the ground both nights. She wrapped her arms around herself to ward off the cold. Their captors discouraged any talk among them, striking the women who disobeyed. In the semidarkness, she examined Kai's foot again, hoping the guards would not see. It had swollen, and red streaks were beginning to spread from the wound. Abigail had tended the sick in Maon and had seen this before on a man who had stepped on a spike while working. The wound festered, and soon he became delirious, sweating profusely. They buried him a week later.

She feared for Kai, but they had no herbs or medicine, little water, and no way to clean the wound. If only it had happened before they crossed the Behor, the cold water would have washed the wound.

At last it seemed the Amalekites were heading toward a large meadow, and they seemed to be stopping. Evidently there was no particular town they were traveling toward. Perhaps their leader was anxious to inventory the spoils they had taken. But if they stopped, what was in store for her and the other women?

The hope that had kept her going these long days was the idea that David would find them and free them from whatever fate these evil men had in store. She had believed that God would deliver them from the battle, one way or another, and that David would return to the burned city of Ziklag and come after them, searching until he found his lost wives and people.

But as they gathered in that grassy meadow, several days' travel from any town or settlement in the vast wilderness, she realized just how hopeless it was. David would never find them. Only Yahweh could help now.

❖

The sun went down, and there were only meager rations for them once again. Abigail tried to give her portion to Ahinoam, but the other woman refused.

"You are good to me," Ahinoam said. "I am thankful. But David would not want you to starve for me. He will want both of his wives healthy when he comes for us."

After the meal, they settled down on the ground and tried to sleep. The grass made the ground a little softer, but the night was cool, and she had only her cloak to cover her.

In the morning, they rose and again ate just enough to keep them from collapsing, though some looked close to that. After they had eaten, the men did not seem to be in any rush, and Abigail eventually realized that they would not be going any farther. The men seemed to be waiting for someone to come and meet them here. The women and children remained tied together in a large group, while the Amalekites waited in the shade of a grove of cypress at the far side of the clearing. The camels and slaves waited a short distance away. Abigail noticed that even the slaves were given shade, while the women were left to bake in the sun. These must not be very good businessmen, Abigail thought. The slave traders would not pay a premium for women who were wilting from the sun's rays and starved.

They passed the day quietly, no one daring to speak too loudly as they sat huddled on the ground. The children begged to get up and run, but their mothers held them in their arms. At one point, someone had started to sing one of the songs David had composed for Yahweh, but one of the Amalekite guards yelled for silence. Abigail tried to think of how she could get them out of this situation.

She worked on the knots that held her to the others, but she could not get them untied. And even if she did manage to break free somehow, where would she go? There were guards stationed around the edges of the group, watching each move they made, and they were at least a day's ride from any settlement. Even if she reached one on foot, she did not know what she would find. It could be worse than whatever fate awaited them here.

That night passed, and another day, and all of them were starting to grow restless. Their captors spent their days going through the goods they had taken from the homes they had raided, appraising each item and counting their newfound wealth. Abigail got the sense that not all the spoils would be delivered to their king.

"If they are going to kill us, why won't they just do it?" Raya asked. "I would rather die than suffer through another day of this misery."

"I believe they are waiting for the slave traders," Abigail said. "This must be where they had agreed to meet them."

"So where are they?" Ahinoam asked, her hand cradling her swollen belly. "Did they get lost? This is miserable."

Abigail knew that as miserable as this was, it was far better than whatever awaited them once the traders arrived. But she bit her tongue, not wanting to worry the other women.

The next morning, Abigail was awakened by a dull rumble, and when she sat up, she could see movement on the horizon. The slave traders were finally arriving, then. She knew it was not a good development, but the monotony of the days of just sitting and waiting was excruciating, as was the hot sun and the meager rations, and she found herself almost grateful for the change.

The approaching horses woke the others, and they sat up and moved closer together. Abigail slipped one arm around Anna and the other around Ahinoam, who was trembling.

They huddled together in fear of what was to come. Several people were praying out loud for Yahweh to deliver them.

But as the horses grew closer, Abigail noticed something strange. The men were not riding slowly and steadily, as would be expected from traders who had traveled a long way. These men were riding at a gallop, closing the distance between themselves and the meadow at breakneck speed. They were also shouting, whooping, and, as they got closer, she saw that they brandished swords.

"Philistines," Anna said, fear choking each syllable.

But Abigail was not so certain. She watched the figures emerge out of the dust, and she tried not to let herself hope. It was hard to tell. They were so far away, and they could be any of dozens of groups who roamed out here in the wilderness. As they grew closer, though, she felt her heart lift. She could start to make out individual figures, and at the front of the group was a big man, riding hard. He was dressed for battle, his dark hair flying back behind him. Was that—

"David!" Ahinoam recognized him just a moment before Abigail.

She hadn't wanted to let herself believe, but it was them. David and his men were coming for them. The Amalekites tried to run when they realized what was happening, but they did not get far. David went straight for the group, followed by half a dozen other men, and Abigail's excitement turned to horror when she saw David swing his sword and take a man's head clean off his shoulders. She heard a chorus of gasps and knew that the others were shocked by the sight as well. But

David had already moved on, and he and his men were running swords through the captors and their slaves. They plowed through the Amalekite warriors like an unstoppable tide.

So this was what David did to the towns he raided. The blood flowed all over the field and the stench that rose to her nostrils made her nauseous. She had only known David the man, the tender lover who laughed with her and shared his thoughts, the leader of the camp. Now as she watched, bile rose up in her throat and she turned away, wanting to stop her ears from the cries of the wounded and dying.

When at last the battle was over, silence reigned over the field. David, along with those men who had women and children, hurried to the clearing to claim their loved ones. Abigail saw him looking for her, and finally their eyes met. She sat quietly, awaiting his approach. Her hair hung down, matted, her face was dirty, and she knew her clothes were in ruins. Next to her stood Ahinoam, just as disheveled.

David turned to Ahinoam first and embraced her. "You are safe. Thanks be to our God, we were in time. Have they hurt you? How is the child?"

"I am fine. The child is fine." Ahinoam shook her head and leaned against him, weeping softly in relief. "I knew you would come for us."

He kissed her on the forehead. "Go with the men. They will provide food for you and the other women and children."

Ahinoam hesitated, and Abigail knew she didn't want to leave him, but she was obedient. With a glance at Abigail, she sighed and left them. When she had gone, David turned to

Abigail and drew her into his arms. She could feel his heart beating rapidly against her.

"Abigail," he said, resting his chin on top of her head. "Are you hurt?"

"No, my lord. Not aside from bruises and the like." She tried to sound more positive than she felt.

"I was so afraid I'd lost you. That I'd lost everything."

"I am so glad you came. I feared—"

"You were right to fear," David said. "These Amalekites have no conscience, no feelings. I am so grateful we found you before..." He leaned down and kissed her cheek, gently. "Before anything bad happened."

Tears formed in her eyes, and the carnage she had witnessed faded into the background in her fierce love for him. "How did you know to come after us? We feared you were deep in battle."

But instead of answering, he kissed her, deeply, hungrily.

"When we return, I will be happy to become more presentable," she managed to say.

"You were never more beautiful to me than you are now." He pulled her close, and she felt herself get lost in his kiss. But the moment was interrupted when David heard someone call his name. He was needed by his people.

Reluctantly, he pulled away and said, "I will tell you all. But first, we must get far from this place. We cannot still be here when the slave traders they were going to meet show up."

The men gathered up the spoils that the Amalekites had taken from Ziklag and the other towns they had raided and loaded them on to the donkeys, horses, and camels. They found far more than just the valuables they had taken from their homes in the Amalekites' things; there were also bags of gold and silver, and many fine jewels. Abigail could not believe the riches that had been traveling with the men. The riches that now belonged to them.

David led the company back in the direction they had come. After the frightening walk that had brought them here, Abigail had not believed she would ever want to walk again, but with every step that took them away from the battlefield they'd left behind brought her a tiny bit more peace. The children and mothers-to-be rode on the horses while the men walked. Kai was also riding on a donkey, her foot so swollen she couldn't put weight on it without crying out. Her skin was flushed and hot, and Abigail feared for her.

That night, they camped on the ground near a stream, lying in the shade of a grove of trees. David made sure the people were settled, and then he took Abigail's arm and led her off, away from the group, into a cave carved into the rock. He brought his torch and held her up as she stumbled down the rock and into the mouth of the cave. He did not even wait until he had set down his torch before his lips were all over her, kissing her mouth, her neck, collarbone. He was tender but eager, and she felt a passion from him that she'd not experienced in some time.

Afterward, they lay on David's cloak on the floor of the cave, watching the light from the torch cast shadows on the walls, shifting and moving as the flames spun and danced.

"Tell me," Abigail said. "How did the Lord keep you from harm? And how did He lead you to where we were?"

"Truly the Lord God was with us," David said. He told her about how he and his men had ridden into Aphek, where the Philistine armies were gathering, and how they were marching with Achish's forces into battle. He recounted how he'd trembled as they walked, fearful that the Lord had not heard his prayers. There seemed to be no way to avoid fighting for the Philistines. But the commander of the Philistines had spotted them and challenged Achish about the Hebrews in their midst. Achish had defended David and his men, saying that he trusted them completely, arguing that this was David, the man Saul sought to kill. But despite the arguments from Achish, the commanders did not trust that David and his men would actually fight for the Philistines when it came down to it.

"He was afraid we would turn on them and fight against the Philistines in an effort to win back Saul's favor," David said. "So we were sent away, not allowed to fight."

Abigail could not believe it. "Yahweh truly did provide," she said. Somewhere in the back of the cave, there was a stream, and she heard water burbling gently over rocks.

"He did." David threaded his fingers through hers. "Just like you said He would."

Abigail said a prayer of thankfulness to the God who protects, for creating a way in an impossible situation. And then, after a moment, she said, "I am surprised they were willing to let over six hundred men just leave a battle."

David shook his head. "There must have been a hundred thousand men fighting for the Philistines. A few hundred will not make any difference in their fight against Saul."

While this was good news for David and his men at the moment, it was a chilling thought. The Philistines were still their enemies. Someday, when David took the throne, he would have to face them again, she was sure. But she would not allow herself to dwell on that for now. Now, she turned onto her side and asked, "So he sent you back to Ziklag?"

"That's right," David said. "But we knew something was wrong well before we arrived back home. We could see the smoke for nearly a day's ride before we found the city still smoldering. We knew something terrible had happened and were only slightly relieved when we could not find anyone left inside. But there were tracks, marks in the sand where it was clear many people had recently walked. So we took off as quickly as we could, hoping to catch you."

"You followed our tracks the whole way?" Abigail could not imagine it. They had walked over large areas of rock. How could his men have found footprints over the rocks?

"No." David shook his head. "We found a young Egyptian slave by the side of the road who had been left there by his Amalekite master. He led us to the camp."

"Oh, you saw him. Will he return with us?"

"Yes, I promised him that. We have no war with the Egyptians."

"The Lord has been gracious," Abigail said.

"The Most High has blessed me mightily," David murmured.

She fell asleep in the crook of his arm. Though they slept on rock, she was so exhausted and so relieved that it felt like the softest feather bed. In the morning, they joined the others. Men were designated to drive the animals and others helped their wives and children. David instructed some of his men to carry the chests and bags of spoils.

Abigail had obtained water for Kai, but she was complaining of pain in her leg and was becoming feverish. Abigail cleaned the wound the best she could and bound it with a clean cloth. Her bag of medicinal herbs had been tucked in a niche in the house in Ziklag. She could only hold a slim hope that the fire had not gotten to it. Kai was put in one of the wagons, and Abigail's other maidservants took turns riding with her and keeping a damp cloth on her head. One of the men gave Yelena a pouch of water for this.

As they walked back toward Ziklag, Abigail thought about what lay ahead. There would be a great deal of rebuilding to do, and Achish would be no help to them, for he and his soldiers were in battle. With a heavy heart, she remembered that the king and the Philistines were battling Israel. She prayed that their people would be victorious, and that the Philistines would never find out David's people were all rooting for them to fail.

◆

Wearily, Abigail and the other women put one foot in front of the other as they returned to Ziklag. Late on the second day of traveling, Anna approached Abigail.

"Mistress?" Anna said quietly. Seeing the look in her eyes, Abigail feared what news she would bring.

"Yes?"

"Mistress, Kai is gone."

Abigail realized she had known what she was going to say, but the words still pierced. "When?"

"She has been hot with fever, tossing and turning, and her leg was terrible to look at. I tried to hold her and comfort her, but she faded away and fell asleep. She stayed that way for an hour or so, but then she stopped breathing."

How could this be? Abigail had just checked on her this morning. Why had no one told her she was getting worse?

"She passed quickly," Anna said. "More quickly than we imagined. But she looked to be at peace."

Abigail was glad, but the words did not help much. She felt tears well up, and suddenly the emotion of the past few days was welling over, tears streaming down her cheeks.

When David heard the news, he stopped the procession. Riding up on his horse, he looked from Abigail's tear-stained face to the body of the young woman two of his men were lifting down from the wagon.

"It is Kai?"

Abigail nodded. David dismounted and put an arm around Abigail's shoulders.

"We will have to bury her here. We don't know what awaits us in Ziklag."

She nodded. "I know." She hated to leave Kai here. "We have no choice."

A grave was dug under a tree in the meadow where they had stopped, and Kai's body was wrapped in a large cloth someone had found among the spoils. It was then lowered gently into the grave.

The people stood around, their heads bowed in respect for the dead as David said a prayer over the grave. Abigail and her other maidservants wept. Kai's warm spirit and friendliness had touched the other women. They and Ahinoam, who had become quite fond of Kai in their time together, wept.

David turned to her. "We need to keep moving, Abigail. We need to reach Ziklag before dark. I'm sorry. I wish I could give you more time."

She nodded. "I understand. We will continue on." There was nothing more she could do for Kai.

They kept moving, but Abigail looked back at the lone grave. Her heart was heavy. She would have to send word to Kai's parents in Maon, if they still lived. She turned her face toward Ziklag.

Abigail wondered what they would do when they reached the town where they had lived. Their homes and possessions had been ravished, and their possessions all dumped together in the spoils. She thought of the rebuilding they would have to do if they were to have any kind of housing.

When they finally approached the town, the people stood for a moment, staring at what was left. The city walls were blackened, and only a few charred roofs still stretched toward the sky. Smoke still rose to the sky in thin gray tendrils, and the smell of ash hung heavy in the air. They went through the ruined gates, twisted and melted, and slowly walked through the town, looking at the damage. Some of the houses had not totally burned, and one by one, families stepped out of the group and set to work to clear out the rubble and clean what was left to make them livable.

The Philistines from Ziklag who had also been captured by the raiders did not return with David's people after they were rescued. When they had been freed along with the other captives, they feared retribution from David and his men and left quickly, and it was believed they headed for other towns in Philistia where they had relatives. David's people would have Ziklag to themselves.

Abigail and Ahinoam and their maidservants stared at the house they had shared. She turned to Ahinoam. "There doesn't seem to be anything left. We have the items the Amalekites took from it, but that is all." The Amalekites had not taken her loom, and she was sure it was now gone.

The people were happy that David had ordered each family to regain what they recognized as their own goods from the plunder taken, so they had some bedding, rugs, and utensils. However, there was no grain for bread. There were only some raisin cakes and some figs.

Faced with six hundred hungry men and their families, David ordered some sheep to be slain and roasted. Some parched grain was recovered from the fields and someone discovered a cache of almonds and two containers of fava beans, which were cut in half and fried. The food the Amalekites had taken was recovered from the containers the raiders had carried away. Everyone contributed what they had found, and the women all worked together to prepare a meal.

When they finally had something to eat, the children stopped crying and each family settled their little ones for sleep on what bedding they had.

David strode back and forth, overseeing the division of the plunder so each family could have their own possessions back. He admonished them to take only what they recognized as their own. "Greed shall not be among us." He told them, "Our God will know if anyone takes what is not his."

He'd given the order that morning; they would begin repairs on the houses at once. Ten men would work on each house until it was habitable, and then they would move on to the next house.

David's quarters had also been mostly destroyed, and he joined some of his men who were single in sleeping on the ground. The men had agreed that as their leader, David's house would be the first one repaired. But there was no access to water yet, as the men were still clearing out the well the Amalekites had filled with stones.

Abigail worked with her maidservants and Ahinoam to make their house livable and clean again, and her thoughts turned to the war now being waged by her people against the Philistines. They had won a temporary reprieve, but if the Philistines won the battle, would David and his people still be welcome in Philistine territory, or would the other kings overrule Achish and take them captive? Or would they be sent back to land held by Israel, where they would be vulnerable to Saul's attacks again? She felt David was also wrestling with these thoughts. His concern had always been the safety of his people. How safe were they, really?

Abigail, Ahinoam, and their maidservants pooled their bedding and slept close to each other for warmth. Abigail lay quietly, her thoughts keeping her awake. She thought of Kai, who had been like a daughter to her. She did everything she knew to do under the circumstances, but she hadn't been able to save her.

She also thought about how she had watched the men slaughter the enemy mercilessly. This was a side of David she had tried not to think about, but she could not avoid it any longer.

She heard the soft snores of the other women and the hooting of an owl outside in the darkness. The birds had survived the fire, she thought. Unlike people, they could fly away to safety, and when the humans had done their damage and gone, the birds quietly returned. Some days Abigail wished that she too could fly away.

She had come a long way from her father's estate. She'd been the wife of a wealthy but brutish husband and then a widow. She had given up life in a big house to marry David and begin a life of constant moving about, hiding from Saul. She found herself wondering—if she'd known what the future held for her, would she still have come?

But she knew the answer was yes. She had known when she answered his invitation to become his wife that she was meant to play some role in the building of Israel. She had assumed it would be by giving David his first son, the heir who would one day become king himself. To be the mother of a king had seemed like the ultimate destiny. But now, these years later, as Ahinoam's belly grew larger each day and David seemed to see Abigail more as an advisor than an object of desire, she wondered if that was to be her role after all. Had God had something else in mind for Abigail in building His kingdom all along?

CHAPTER TWENTY

◆

As the new day dawned, Abigail woke, and hearing voices outside, she realized people were already up and about, beginning work. She rose and dressed quickly. She needed to see what could be put together for a morning meal for the camp. Men and women went outside the city to see what else could be gleaned from the fields and fruit trees. Anything edible was carefully gathered in shawls and baskets. In the meantime, the first group of men began work, first on the houses most salvageable. They had also begun working on David's quarters. Women swept with makeshift brooms made from some straw they tied to a branch and secured with a leather thong. Other men climbed down the well and stood in the remaining water to hand up stones to those above to clear the well.

The women could hardly wait to have water to wash in again. Any water brought from the creek was carefully parceled out.

David sorted through the plunder that had been taken from other towns. Abigail suggested he send part of it to each of the elders of Judah, along with the words, "Here is a present for you, taken from the Lord's enemies." As he gave the names, Abigail wrote the list on a scroll of the towns that David had visited that had helped them. Gifts were prepared and sent by groups of his warriors to each of the towns.

When the men and women had been working on Ziklag for a week, a man arrived. He had torn his clothes and put dirt on his head to show he was in mourning. His horse was lathered from the long ride.

David went to meet him, and the camp gathered around the man, anxious to hear what news he brought. After some water and bread, the man gathered his strength and shook his head.

"Where have you come from?" David asked.

"I came from the Israelite camp."

Abigail saw several men shift on their feet. This man was not an Israelite. Why had he come here? But David was more interested in a different question. He put a hand on the man's shoulder. "What happened? Tell me how the battle went."

"Our entire army fled from the battle." So this man claimed the Israelite army as his own, then, Abigail thought.

"Many of our men are dead. Saul and his sons, including Jonathan, are also dead. When the army saw that the king was dead, they ran away. Then when the people on the other side of the Jezreel Valley and beyond the Jordan heard the news, they abandoned their towns and fled. The Philistines now occupy those towns."

Abigail felt the air go out of her lungs. Their people had lost. They had run away from the fight. They had been conquered by the Philistines.

She could see on the faces of the men and women around her that they were as devastated by the news as she was. Channah had to hold Ahinoam up so she didn't fall over. How had Yahweh allowed such a thing to happen?

But even in her devastation, in her confusion and pain, Abigail felt something else. A glimmer of an idea, hovering just around the edges of her mind.

"How do you know Saul and Jonathan are dead?" David demanded. His face was twisted in pain. Jonathan had been his dearest friend, and despite Saul's behavior in recent years, he had once been like a father to David.

"I saw it myself," the young man said. "I happened to be on Mount Gilboa and there was Saul, leaning on his spear with the enemy chariots closing in on him."

"His sons were already dead?" David asked.

"I am afraid so. Abinadab was lying nearby, and the others were not far away, but we had heard that they were gone as well."

"Saul was able to pierce his side with his spear?" David asked, pain clouding his features.

"He was too weak," the young man said. "He was in so much pain, but he could not do it on his own. So he called me and begged me to put him out of his misery."

"So what did you do?" David watched the young man carefully.

"I obeyed the king," he said. "What else could I do? He could not live much longer. It seemed an act of mercy."

As David heard the words, his face changed.

"I brought these for you," the young man said, and when he reached into his bag, he pulled out the king's crown and armband. "I am told you are the one the Lord has chosen to be king."

Instead of taking the crown and armband, David tore his clothes, and his men did the same thing. He turned and walked

Pursued by a King: Abigail's Story

away, vanishing into the shell of his home, half laid with new timber. Abigail knew that he was mourning for his friend Jonathan. After he disappeared, two of his men took the young man away until David could tell them what to do with him. David did not come out of his shelter all that day and most of the next. He sat by himself mourning, and his men mourned and fasted all day also.

When evening came on the second day, David rose and called for the young man who had brought them the news. Abigail watched the confrontation from the street.

"Where are you from?" David asked.

"I am an Amalekite, who lives in your land."

The look on David's face was terrible to see. "What made you think it was all right for you to kill the Lord's anointed one?"

"He was dying already. I only helped him because he was in pain," the man insisted.

But David shook his head. "It is not for any man to shed the blood of the Lord's anointed king."

For a moment, Abigail thought David was simply going to walk away. She hoped that he would let him go, that recent events might have softened the heart of her warrior husband.

But then, he turned to one of his men. "Kill him," he said quietly.

It gave him no joy to give the order, Abigail saw, but he had no choice. The young man shrieked and started to argue, but the sound was cut off when David's man thrust his sword into the man's side.

"You have condemned yourself," David said to the dying man, "for you yourself confessed that you had killed the Lord's anointed one."

David then left the assembled crowd. Abigail knew he was mourning and needed to get away. She let him go. He needed to be alone.

She left him alone for two days, listening, as the whole group did, to the mournful notes that drifted out of his home. She heard the talk of the men who tried to figure out how to help, what they should do. She waited. When she could stand it no more, she dressed in her finest robe, combed out her hair, and walked toward his home.

What she was about to do was foolishness, she knew. She could not approach him without being summoned. It was not done, especially with someone of David's stature. It was foolish, and could result in David's anger and retribution.

Then again, it was an act of what most would have called foolishness that had brought her into David's path in the first place. It was her bravery, her willingness to face her problems head-on, that had saved herself and her household and had led to her marriage to David. He had claimed he valued her for her bravery. She would see now if he still did.

When Abigail approached the door of David's house, she heard him singing softly, strumming the lyre gently.

Your pride and joy, O Israel, lies dead on the hills!

He sang, his voice clear and strong.
    Oh, how the mighty heroes have fallen!
Don't announce the news in Gath,
    don't proclaim it in the streets of Ashkelon,

or the daughters of the Philistines will rejoice
>   and the pagans will laugh in triumph.

O mountains of Gilboa,
>   let there be no dew or rain upon you,
>   nor fruitful fields producing offerings of grain.

For there the shield of the mighty heroes was defiled;
>   the shield of Saul will no longer be anointed with oil.

The bow of Jonathan was powerful,
>   and the sword of Saul did its mighty work.

They shed the blood of their enemies
>   and pierced the bodies of mighty heroes.

How beloved and gracious were Saul and Jonathan!
>   They were together in life and death.

They were swifter than eagles,
>   stronger than lions.

O women of Israel, weep for Saul,
>   for he dressed you in luxurious scarlet clothing,
>   in garments decorated with gold.

Oh, how the mighty heroes have fallen in battle!
>   Jonathan lies dead on the hills.

How I weep for you, my brother Jonathan!
>   Oh, how much I loved you!

And your love for me was deep,
>   deeper than the love of women!

Oh, how the mighty heroes have fallen!
>   Stripped of their weapons, they lie dead.

It was beautiful and haunting, and Abigail let the last notes fade away before she knocked on the door.

"My lord?" she called.

There was a pause, and then, "Abigail?"

She pushed open the door and stepped inside the room. It was hot in here, and stuffy, stinking of sweat.

"What are you doing here?"

"I came to see you," Abigail said. "It is important."

David watched her, waiting for her to go on. He might be angry with her impertinence, but he had not thrown her out yet.

"I am sorry about the death of King Saul," Abigail said.

He nodded.

"But I am wondering what you will do now."

"What do you mean, what I will do?" His face was pale, and his hair hung in greasy hanks.

"I mean, there is not much time."

"Time for what?"

"Before someone else marches into Gibeah and claims control of Israel."

"There is no Israel anymore. Did you not hear? The Philistines have taken the land."

"They have only taken a portion of our territory, and the Lord gave it to our people. You are a mighty warrior." She stepped toward him. "Go get it back."

His eyes widened, and he reared back as if she had hit him.

"You are the Lord's chosen," she continued. She needed to get this out before he threw her out, or worse. "You have always said your desire is to see the Lord's presence dwell in your palace. You were going to be the one to bring the Ark of the Covenant where it belongs. Now is your chance. Will you stay here and hide out among your enemies, or will you ride into Israel and claim your throne?"

David looked at her but did not speak. He seemed to be weighing his response. Abigail heard only the sound of her ragged breathing. She forced herself to stand steady and clasped her hands together so he would not see them tremble. Finally, he set the lyre down, pushed himself up, and spoke: "Go."

Abigail turned and hurried out of the house, her feet carrying her quickly through the streets, which still smelled of charred wood and ash, until she got back to the house she shared with Ahinoam. They had cleared out one room, and Ahinoam lay on a mat next to the wall, facing the wall, clutching her belly.

Abigail waited, on edge, all the rest of that day and into the next. At every sound, she expected soldiers to come to her door and drag her out into the street. She kept thinking that David's men would show up to punish her for her impertinence, and for her foolishness. But no one came.

The next morning, all of David's people were summoned, and they gathered to hear what he would say.

As soon as David emerged from his home, her heart lifted. She saw immediately that his countenance had changed. His eyes were alight with anticipation as he waited for his people to quiet.

"My friends, I am pleased to say that the Lord has directed us to go to Hebron."

Abigail gazed at David's advisors Ishbaal and Eleazar and saw that she was not the only one who was puzzled by the city the Lord had chosen. Hebron was in the land given to the tribe of Judah—David's tribes and hers—and David would no doubt find much support there. But the center of Saul's empire had been in Gibeah. True, that city was in the hands of the Philistines now, but if David was to claim his throne, shouldn't they be headed there to take it back? Why were they heading to Hebron?

However, among the bulk of the crowd, there was a surge of excitement, and there were even a few shrieks as people realized what this meant. Hebron! The word was joyfully passed from family to family as excitement began to build. They would be leaving the land of the Philistines and going into the territory of Judah, their own homeland.

David continued, shouting, "We will return to Israel at last."

CHAPTER TWENTY-ONE

Less than a week later, the group approached the gates of the city of Hebron. As they neared, a group of men came out to meet them. Abigail saw that it was a delegation of elders.

David dismounted and waited for them to approach. The leader bowed low to David. "I am Simon, head of the council of elders. We welcome God's anointed to our city."

David smiled at the words. It had been an empty phrase for him for fifteen years. "We are happy to be here. As you can see, I have a large number of people with me. Can you accommodate them?"

"Most assuredly. We are well prepared for you and your followers. There are several small towns around Hebron, and we have arranged for your people to settle there."

David gestured to Abigail and Ahinoam to come forward. "These are my wives, Abigail and Ahinoam."

The men bowed. "We welcome you also," said Simon. He smiled at Ahinoam. "There will soon be a child."

Indeed, it would not be long now. The journey had been difficult on Ahinoam. Truthfully, it had not been easy for Abigail either. The swaying of the donkey underneath her had made her feel nauseous, and she was exhausted and her breasts tender. But all of that would remain her secret for now. She had seen that David did not call for Ahinoam at night once he had learned she was with child, and Abigail wanted to keep David close to her.

"A boy, I am sure of it." David beamed at Ahinoam. "The first of many."

"I have no doubt." Simon nodded.

David became serious. "It has been many years since the prophet Samuel anointed me as the next king. Someone already held that position."

Simon nodded. "Yes. We were loyal to Saul for that reason. He was the first anointed king. Now he is dead, and we are without a king to lead us." He looked back at the other elders, and they all nodded their heads. Simon turned back to David.

"You are the one God chose to succeed Saul, and it is time you were able to take your rightful place. We are prepared to offer you the kingship over the land of Judah."

Over *Judah*? Just the southern portion of the kingdom? Why not over all Israel? Abigail looked at David, but he did not seem confused by the turn of events.

"The Lord is good, and has His own timing for everything. He has sent me here, and told me what awaited me. Therefore, I accept."

The elders were obviously relieved. "Come, let us escort you, your wives, and your people to our city." Many of those who had families in the area had already broken off, and others would be assigned to cities to make their home within the region. But for now, those that remained with David followed him into the city.

A runner had been sent ahead to announce his coming, and when they entered the city the people lined the streets. Hebron was a wealthy city, full of powerful men, and all the people came out and cheered and threw flowers at David, crying out,

"Hail to our new king!

"God's anointed. May you be blessed!"

"Welcome to King David!"

Abigail and Ahinoam rode behind David on horses donated by two of his men. Abigail tugged at the disheveled clothing they wore. Her other clothes had burned with their house in Ziklag. She certainly didn't feel like a wife of a king.

The procession wound around the streets to a beautiful and stately home, high on a hill. David paused for a moment and looked at her, just the hint of a smile on his face.

❖

Abigail looked up at the imposing structure before them. It had been a private home owned by a wealthy man and his many wives, but it had been donated to house David's family now.

A man met them at the entrance and bowed low. "I am Nour, steward to the previous owner of this home. I will serve you as I served my master."

He nodded to some waiting servants, who led Abigail and Ahinoam to their quarters. Anna, Talia, and Yelena followed their mistress, while Channah followed Ahinoam, who fairly waddled as she walked.

Abigail found her quarters quite to her liking. The room was as large as the main bedroom in Maon. There was a window that looked down on the courtyard, and an oil lamp on an ornate table by a large, comfortable bed. Thick rugs had been laid on the stone floor and there was a small table and chair by the window. Sunlight poured into the room through the window, lending warmth and cheer to the room.

The room had been recently cleaned in preparation for their arrival, so she set her servants to work looking into any storage room for some clothing for her. Everything she owned had been lost in Ziklag, even her treasured loom and yarns. David had promised her that when they were settled in Hebron, he would have another one made for her. She would hold him to that promise.

Yelena opened a chest at the foot of the bed and exclaimed, "Mistress! Here are some clothes for you!"

Anna and Talia hurried over, and they spread out the contents on the bed. There were two gowns and some gold slippers. Abigail tried on both dresses. To her amazement, they fit her fairly well. The dresses would do for now, but she would send to her father for the rest of her clothes.

"Mistress, come and see!" Anna stood in a small doorway that opened off the bedroom. "A pool for bathing!"

Indeed, it was the most wonderful thing Abigail had beheld in a long time. The small pool was elevated so wood could be placed underneath to heat the water. There was also a small stall with a hole in the stone floor for taking care of other needs. Abigail shook her head in amazement.

Her three servants found the small room they were to occupy supplied with bedding. There was also a table and a small oil lamp. Abigail told Anna to find Nour and see if there was any other clothing. Her maids would need clothes too.

There was a knock on the door and two male servants came in with wood to start the fire under the pool. Another servant arrived with clean garments for her three maids. She smiled. When the fire was going well, the men bowed and left.

After she had bathed in the warm water, Abigail donned a thin tunic Anna had found in the chest and had the best night's sleep she could remember.

CHAPTER TWENTY-TWO

The next morning, Abigail stretched and looked around the room, for a moment expecting to see the burned walls of their house in Ziklag. Then she remembered where she was. Her tattered dress from the night before was gone. When Talia and Yelena brought her some fruit, goat cheese, and some freshly baked bread, she realized they had taken advantage of the bathing room also, and were clad in clean garments.

Anna entered with a smile on her face. She carried a gown of soft blue with gold embroidered along the sleeves. "Nour sent this to you, mistress, to wear for the coronation ceremony. It will be today. Nour will come for you."

Today? David would be crowned King of Judah today!

Abigail admired the beautiful gown and wondered where Nour had gotten it. Perhaps she could ask him about other clothes.

Yelena dressed her, and Talia combed Abigail's hair and plaited it to wind around her head. She had the pouch of jewelry she'd carried under her clothes, and a few pieces of her jewelry had been recovered from the plunder. She had been able to recognize these pieces when the jewelry was spread out. Some of her jewelry had no doubt been claimed by other women, but there was nothing she could do about that now.

She put on a pair of gold earrings and a gold pendant on a chain around her neck.

Nour came for her, and when they entered the hall, she met Ahinoam. She was no doubt also wearing a borrowed dress. "You slept well, Ahinoam?"

"Yes, my quarters are quite comfortable." She nodded to Abigail. "It is good to sleep in a bed again."

Later, Talia told Abigail that she'd spoken with Channah and was told that Ahinoam's quarters were slightly larger and more luxurious. It was only right, Abigail reasoned, since Ahinoam was David's wife before her and she was expecting David's firstborn.

As they entered the great hall, Abigail could hear that the city was alive with singing and dancing. The celebration of their new king had begun.

She and Ahinoam were led to the dais and seated on thrones, Ahinoam on the right of David's throne and Abigail next to her, as they waited for David to make his appearance.

All the elders and nobles of Hebron were assembled on either side of the entrance. The men who had followed David all through the years came from the villages assigned them to see their beloved leader crowned king.

Trumpets were sounded and drums beat a steady rhythm as he walked from the entrance of the great hall, toward the dais, and ascended the steps to his throne. His hair had been washed and trimmed, as had his beard. Nour must have also found clothes for him, for he was regally dressed. To Abigail's eyes, he looked every inch a king, and more handsome than ever.

Abiathar, the young priest who had survived Saul's slaughter of the priests and their families, walked behind David. He wore a new ephod. As the one representative of the priesthood until more could be chosen from the lineage of Aaron, he stood proudly and prayed before placing the crown upon David's head.

Ahinoam would now be Queen of Judah, while she herself was placed as his second wife. Abigail tried to push down the jealousy that threatened to rise up. She must let Ahinoam take her place of honor.

Abiathar spread his hands toward the assembled dignitaries. "I give you David, the anointed King of Judah!"

With one voice the crowd rose up to cry out, "Hail, David, King of Judah!"

As pleased as Abigail was, she was still confused about why David was only being crowned ruler of the southern part of Saul's kingdom.

A great banquet was held, with roasted lamb seasoned with cumin, grilled quail, many bowls of grapes and plums, goat stew with squash and olives, raisin cakes, and honey-almond stuffed dates. David's people had not eaten so well in a very long time, and David made sure the wine flowed freely to those who had been so loyal to him all through these past years.

"Abigail. My beloved." David came up and slipped his arm around her waist. "Are you happy tonight?" He was flushed from dancing.

"I am happy, my lord."

"Something is troubling you. What can be upsetting you, tonight of all nights? You are married to a king!"

"I know, my lord. I am pleased for you."

"Does the palace not suit? Do you desire larger quarters?"

"My quarters are wonderful."

"But…"

He had had much wine, but he still had his wits about him. Abigail decided to take the opportunity to ask about what was truly troubling her.

"Why were you crowned king over Judah only? The Lord anointed you to be king over all of Israel, didn't he?"

"He did." David sobered, turning to face her. "You are really incredible, do you know that? Not many wives would be worried about these things. They would simply be enjoying heated baths and rich food."

Abigail thought he was underestimating the minds of most women, but she did not say so. She waited for him to go on.

"You know that Saul and three of his sons were killed at Mount Gilboa."

Abigail nodded.

"His remaining son, Ish-Bosheth, backed by Saul's former commander, Abner, has claimed the throne of Israel. He has established his palace in Mahanaim."

Abigail sucked in a breath. Mahanaim was outside the territory that had been claimed by the Philistines. "But he cannot be king. You are the one the Lord ordained to be king over Israel."

"And so it will be," David said. "One day, Abigail. Someday, it will be just as we imagined. We will build a kingdom that serves Yahweh first, and His reign will have no end."

"But not now," Abigail said. She had thought they were finally to claim what the Lord promised.

"It appears that the Lord has other plans for us for now."

Abigail knew what this meant. It meant many years of war, of seeing her husband lead his armies into battle not just against the enemies of the Hebrews, but against their own people in an effort to claim the throne over the north as well. David would not rest until he had fulfilled the Lord's calling on his life, she knew this. And yet she dreaded what lay ahead.

"You will need many allies for this fight," she said.

David did not answer for a moment. He was thinking, his brow furrowed. "More allies?"

"You already have the support of the rulers of the towns in Judah, but you will need to build support from neighboring nations if you intend to fight Saul's son."

Then David threw back his head and laughed. "Abigail. My Abigail. You are precious to me, and worth more than all of my advisors."

She let a smile spread across her face. She reached out and touched his arm. "I am also prettier, am I not?"

Instead of answering, he leaned in and kissed her.

"My Abigail. You are right, as always. But please, do not worry about allies and such things tonight," he said. "Tonight, we celebrate. Yahweh is faithful. What He has ordained will come to pass. Do you remember how He protected us all of those years in the wilderness?"

"I do." She smiled, thinking back to that road in the night time where she'd first met her husband. "You were not the only one He protected."

"He is faithful. Let us keep the faith as well. This is not the kingdom we imagined yet. But this is the first step."

David's face glowed as he rejoiced in all that the Lord had done for him, and he danced with abandon. The people celebrated all that day and into the night, and even though David wasn't yet king over all Israel, Abigail rejoiced, because the Lord had blessed her mightily. She was married to the king, the most handsome man in the land, and she had a baby on the way, though no one knew her secret yet. And when David called for her that night, it was clear that he loved her and took great joy in her.

Soon, the visitors came. Kings of neighboring nations came to bring their best wishes to David. The first was Talmai, the king of Geshur, who arrived, he said, with a gift to solidify their alliance. Abigail was stunned when the "gift" turned out to be the king's daughter, Maacah. She could be no more than eighteen, her long black hair hanging down her back and her dark eyes accented with kohl.

She was quite beautiful and obviously very impressed with David. Abigail saw that David was also pleased with Talmai's daughter. He signed a treaty with Talmai and then announced to the elders that he was taking Maacah as his wife.

As soon as it was proper, Abigail excused herself. With a last look at David, who was absorbed in his new acquisition, she went to her quarters. Her heart felt like a stone in her chest.

A wedding celebration was held for several days, but neither Abigail nor Ahinoam attended. And neither of them were called to David for many weeks.

Not long after the marriage, Abigail heard yelling, following by a deep-throated moaning, as she passed the door to Ahinoam's chambers. Abigail knew what it meant. Ahinoam was having the child. Abigail knocked gently on the door, and Channah opened it a crack. "I was hoping you were the midwife," Channah said. "She is much delayed, and the mistress is in great pain."

"I have some herbs that may help," Abigail said. She went to her chambers and found the herbs she'd found among the ashes at Ziklag. Some had escaped the fire, and she brought the herbs to Ahinoam now. As they waited for the midwife to arrive, she put cold cloths on Ahinoam's head when she was laid down in between contractions. Ahinoam did not speak to her, but her eyes told Abigail she was grateful for the comfort.

She screamed in pain, but it took six hours after the midwife arrived before Ahinoam's son was born. The king had a crown prince. David entered the chamber as soon as the midwife allowed him to and was given the baby to hold. His pride was shown in his large grin as he looked down at the tiny form.

Then he announced, "He shall be called Amnon, faithful and true."

He comforted Ahinoam and then was finally convinced to let her rest. With a glance back at his new son, he left, but reluctantly.

Ahinoam nursed her baby and looked at Abigail, who had stayed with her through the whole ordeal.

"Thank you, Abigail," she said. "I pray that you too shall bear a son."

Abigail was surprised but pleased to hear the words. She admired little Amnon but knew that his birth meant that even if she had a boy, he would never be king.

❖

Many weeks later Abigail stood at her window looking down at the courtyard. Tears threatened to slip down her cheeks, and she brushed them away. She felt nauseous, and some days she was too exhausted to even get out of bed. She grew more and more frustrated by the day. There had been little to do but read some of the scrolls of the Talmud Talia found for her in the palace and walk in the inner garden. David had finally procured another loom for her, and she spent much time weaving her linen, but there were only so many blankets one could need. There were no other women to talk with besides her three maidservants and Ahinoam, who seldom came out of her room. David was occupied with his new wife, and also with amassing alliances to be able to fight Ish-Bosheth to take Israel as well as Judah. The worst part was knowing that she had not told David about the life growing inside her so that he would continue to call to her, but he called Maacah instead. She needed to find a way to get back into his good graces.

It was more than a week later that Anna came into her chambers with a message. "The king calls for you, mistress. He sent word for you to come to him." Nour waited outside her door.

Abigail's heart leaped. David had remembered her. She was not cast aside. She prepared herself and quickly followed the steward through the halls of the palace, lit with candles and torches against the evening gloom, to the king's quarters.

Nour bowed and left, closing the door behind him. David was sitting behind a table that was strewn with papers. Abigail waited quietly for David to speak.

"Abigail. I wanted to ask your opinion on a matter."

"My opinion, my lord?" She tried not to let her disappointment show. There were many people who could give him an opinion. She was his wife. It had been many weeks since she had seen him.

"You always see things more clearly than my advisors."

He should look into getting some new advisors, she thought, but she bit her tongue.

"What is the matter that you need my thoughts on?" Abigail asked.

"As you have suggested, I need to form alliances with neighboring kingdoms," David said.

Abigail already regretted the day she had given David those words of advice, seeing that the alliance with the Geshurites had resulted in Maacah. Now she feared what he was going to say.

"An emissary from the Amalekites is due to arrive here in the next day," David said. "And the following week, the Girzites will be arriving."

Abigail hated the thought of any member of the Amalekite tribe setting foot in Hebron after what they had done to her and the other Hebrew women.

"The two groups hate one another, and I fear they will not join me if they have heard that I am aligned with the other. Which do you think is more valuable?"

"Both," she said without hesitation. She did not understand much of the negotiating and jockeying for position that went on about leading kingdoms, but she did understand simple math. "You need as many allies as possible to overcome Ish-Bosheth."

"But how can I have both, if they will not work together?" David asked.

"I do not know, my lord. I am sure you will find a way. But if you want my advice, there it is. Do not choose. Have both."

David was quiet for a moment, and then, slowly, he nodded his head, just a bit. "It is an interesting approach."

"What do your advisors say?"

"Some say that Amalekites are more important, others the Girzites. You are the first to suggest I should not have to choose."

"You are the Lord's anointed," she said. "What He has promised, He will fulfill." Abigail said it because it was true, and also because David, like a child, loved to hear about his own importance.

"Thank you, Abigail." He called for Nour and looked back down at his parchments. While the door creaked open, Abigail stepped back toward David.

"Is there anything else you need, my lord?" She tugged down the neckline of her robe.

He did not look up from his parchment. "No, thank you, Abigail. That is all." He gestured for Nour to see her out and then, almost as an afterthought, called after Nour, "And have Maacah sent over."

Abigail bit her lip to prevent tears from rising. He may value her judgment, but she had lost her place as his favorite wife, that much was clear. Young Maacah had taken her place in his bed. But Abigail lifted her chin. She was not going to give in that easily.

"My lord?" she said brightly. "I almost forgot to tell you my news."

"What news?" David looked up when she circled back toward him.

Nour hovered next to her, clearly unsure what he should do.

"I am going to have a child," she said.

"You are with child?" He dropped the parchments. "Really?"

"Yes, my lord."

"That is very good news indeed." He stood up, hurried to her, and gathered her to him. He murmured in her ear, "I am glad, beloved. It has always been my prayer that you bear me a son." He rubbed his hand across her belly, just starting to become round, and smiled.

She leaned back and smiled up at him. "I cannot guarantee that it will be a boy."

"I will love it whether it is a girl or a boy. Just as I love its beautiful mother." As David pulled her in for a long kiss, she knew she had calculated correctly.

◆

David showed Abigail special favor for the next few weeks, sending her special treats of honeyed figs and salty cheese, but it did not take long for his attention to fade, largely due to the arrival of two new wives. Shortly after the visit from the king of the Amalekites, David married a beautiful woman with hair to her trim waist and a husky, smoky voice. She was named Abital, a gift from their king. Soon afterward, David was presented with Haggith, whose face was perhaps the most beautiful Abigail had ever seen. This, apparently, was how David had been able to solidify alliances with the two enemy tribes.

As the weeks went by and they both fell farther out of the king's favor, Abigail and Ahinoam grew closer. They spent many hours together, talking while Ahinoam fed Amnon. Ahinoam shared the larger robes she had worn during her pregnancy as Abigail's time progressed. Ahinoam was perhaps not Abigail's first choice of companion, but they were bound by what they had suffered together through the wandering years. These newer wives, who got to enjoy warm baths and clean linens during their bridal weeks, could not even begin to understand what Abigail and Ahinoam had been through.

Abigail's time came in the fall when the grapes were being harvested. She looked forward to the birth with mixed emotions, remembering her ordeal years before.

She did not deliver her son quickly this time either. The baby was feet first, and the local midwife had to turn him. The pain was excruciating, and she bit down hard on the rag Anna had given her. After many hours of hard labor and pain so powerful she thought she would not make it, she felt the child slide from her body. She fell down against the bed, and the midwife held up the baby. He was covered in a thick slime, but he was not gray like her first.

"You have a son, mistress!" Anna crowed.

After the long labor, Abigail was bone weary. She had lost much blood. The midwife was finally able to stop the bleeding using a strong poultice of herbs.

"He has torn you badly, my lady," the midwife murmured, "You may not be able to bear any more children. Another child could take your life. This one nearly did."

As she cradled her small son and held him close to nurse, she decided it did not matter. She had a living child this time, and it was David's.

After the midwife had cleaned up the room and Abigail had put on a fresh robe, David burst in and strode over to Abigail. He bent over to kiss her forehead. "You have given me a fine son." He looked down at his second child with love and pride. "Did I not tell you it would be a boy?" he exalted. "He shall be called Chileab."

The name meant "restraint of father" and Abigail wondered at the choice. The baby breathed with effort and did not seem strong, but the midwife assured her he would get stronger—he'd just had a hard time coming into the world.

"Rest, beloved," David kissed her forehead again and touched her cheek with his hand before leaving. Abigail felt she would burst with happiness. The Lord had lifted His hand and blessed her with a son. She could ask for nothing more.

CHAPTER TWENTY-THREE

Chileab was a wonderful baby, happy and smiling and the very image of his father. Abigail had never known love like she felt when she looked at his tiny squished-up face, his little perfect fingers. The duties of motherhood consumed her, and she fell blissfully under its spell. She rejoiced in her son's first steps, his first words, the curls of his hair, and the feel of his heartbeat against her own. The Lord had blessed her.

Chileab was now in his third year. Butterflies were a matter of wonder. He could sit on the grass and watch them, waving his small hands at them, talking in unintelligible syllables to them. Once, when one landed on a flower near him, he reached for it only to have it fly away. As his face clouded up with the threat of tears, she distracted him with the sighting of a small line of bugs crawling along a leaf. This also required intense concentration. He seemed to realize they were too small to pick up, but watched their progress happily. He was not a robust child, thinner than she wished, but he seemed healthy.

Sometimes Ahinoam brought Amnon to play with him, but Abigail was not pleased on these occasions. Amnon was a spoiled child, indulged to the point of petulance if something did not go his way. Once he had pushed Chileab down on the grass and taken away a toy Chileab was playing with. Talia and

Yelena hesitated to interfere, as Amnon was the crown prince. Abigail had no hesitation about stepping in and restoring the toy to her son. Ahinoam had Channah pick up her son, and they promptly left the garden, but not without Ahinoam giving Abigail a withering look. When it came to her child, friendship was set aside. Amnon's lower lip protruded as he scowled at them over Channah's shoulder.

Abigail seldom encountered the other wives and their children, and she was relieved that she didn't. There seemed to be an unspoken agreement that they were not in the garden at the same time as Ahinoam and Abigail.

Anna had developed severe health problems, and her hands and back ached a great deal. Her fingers began to become malformed. Abigail watched Anna's face as she did small chores and the pain of her hands was obvious. She did not complain, but one day Abigail called her faithful nurse to her.

"Anna, are you in pain? Your hands seem to trouble you."

"Not just my hands, mistress, but my knees. The potions from the healer do not seem to help."

"Where would you go if I released you, Anna?"

The woman's eyes grew wide. "You would send me away, mistress?"

Abigail smiled. "Only if you have a safe place to go. Do you have any family left?"

"I have an older brother and his family. His children are grown, but there are nieces and nephews. I have heard from him occasionally. I believe I would be welcome there. We are family."

Abigail put a gentle hand on the older woman's shoulder. "I do not wish to see you suffer, Anna. Write to your brother, and if you are welcome, I will release you."

Anna bowed her head. "You are a generous and kind woman, mistress. There is no one like you in the entire palace. You have endured much, and you have risen above your sorrow." With tears in her eyes, she nodded. "I will send word to my brother."

It did not take long for word to come back to Anna that her brother and family would be glad to see her again, and she would be welcome in their home. It was a sad day for Abigail watching Anna pack her few belongings. Anna had been like a mother to her.

Talia and Yelena wept as they embraced Anna, and large tears rolled down Chileab's face when he realized his Anna was leaving him. She had been like his *savta,* the grandmother he never knew.

When Anna had gone, taken in a cart guarded by two soldiers David had ordered to see her safely to her brother's home, Abigail put her hand to her chest. Her heart was heavy with her sense of loss. First Kai, and now Anna.

Abigail pushed the thoughts aside and looked over at Talia and Yelena, who were tossing a ball of string with Chileab. His childish laughter rang out in the garden, and she realized that though life was not all she wished, she had found contentment in her son.

David had taken another wife, Eglah, and several of his wives had now given him sons. He was busy with his many wives and his machinations against Abner and Ish-Bosheth. He had called Abigail to him several times to ask her opinion on a matter, though she was less interested than ever in the war games played by men. Her advice to David was always the same: trust in the Lord to fulfill His promises. She would not give him any more specific advice than that. She had learned her lesson. Sometimes she felt sad, remembering the days when he couldn't keep his hands off her, but she knew she was lucky to be in a position where he valued her opinion.

Since she was no longer needed on a nightly basis, Abigail had asked David for permission to go home to Carmel and visit her father, who had yet to meet his grandson. David refused, saying that he wanted to keep his sons near and also that he needed Abigail in case a matter came up and he needed her opinion. She was flattered, but inside she grieved. Was she a prisoner in this palace? For all David's words about valuing her above his advisors, she was still at the mercy of her husband's will.

After many messages back and forth to her father, it was decided that he would leave his business for a time and come to visit Abigail in Hebron. Abigail prepared her quarters and put on her best robe, anxiously waiting for him to arrive. Finally Nour came to find her in the garden one day. "Your visitor has arrived, my lady."

She looked up and saw her father walking slowly down the path of the garden. His hair was now more gray than black, and fine lines marked his face. His nose was marred by many fine red lines. Was her father in his fifties now, or sixties? For a moment she felt like a child again, wanting to run and fling herself into his arms as she'd done long ago. Instead, she rose and smiled at him.

"Abba! How good to see you."

"It is good to see you, my Abigail." He held her tightly and then pulled back and gazed at her. "I have missed you."

"And I you."

"Look at you. Married to a king. Living in a palace." He shook his head.

Her father then turned to see the little boy staring up at him in confusion.

"And this must be Chileab." He crouched down and looked the child in the eye. "Hello, Chileab. I am your *sabba*."

Chileab cried and hid behind his mother's skirts.

"Chileab!" Abigail gasped, but her father laughed.

"He is just as you were at that age."

He embraced her and then looked at Chileab. "David is pleased with his son?"

"Oh yes. He is a fine boy."

"He seems thin. Does he get enough to eat?"

She had to laugh. "Yes, Abba, he gets enough to eat." Then she sobered. "He was ill for a while, but he is better now."

He gave her a smile. "And what about you? Before David was crowned, it must have been difficult."

She thought of the hectic life in the camp, constantly packing up and moving to avoid Saul. Then there were the Amalekite raiders. How could she tell him how close she came to being a slave or worse? She decided it was easier not to go into all that. "It was difficult at times but had its rewards. It was certainly not boring. We did travel a great deal."

"I listened to the reports that carried from town to town. I did not try to dissuade you from your choice to follow David. It has brought you here. I just wanted you to be happy."

"I am happy." She looked past him, toward the tree branches that danced gently in the breeze.

"And David. Is he satisfied with his life?"

Abigail did not know how to answer the question. "He is troubled by Abner, the commander of Saul's army." Abigail knew that there had been several battles between the two armies, and they had caused much bloodshed but no real progress.

"The man standing between David and the throne of Israel."

"That is right."

"It was God's plan long ago, Daughter, that your husband ascend the throne. He was not anointed just to be king of Judah, but of all Israel. What the Lord God ordains will come to pass, but in His time, not ours."

"Yes, I know. That is what I tell David too."

He watched Chileab for a while. "I wish you could visit me in the country. The fresh air would be good for my grandson."

Abigail shook her head. "I have asked, but David won't let us leave. He loves having his sons near him." And then she added, "And I would not leave my son."

Her father did not answer, but there was something in his gaze.

"What is it?"

"I dare not say. He is our king."

"Now you must say."

"It is just that he seems very much like a child. Wanting things his way all the time."

Abigail hated to think it, but she could see certain resemblances to Chileab's behavior in David's own. Always desiring something new, something better, and inconsolable if he could not have it. She decided to change the subject.

"How are things at home? Is your steward still with you?"

"He is, but getting older, like me. The aches and pains increase."

She felt a stab of fear. Somehow knowing Remiel was at her former home had been comforting.

"Do not forget, Abigail, that you are my only child. Since I have no son, by the law passed down from Moses, you inherit my property. My home is still yours, and one day you will have to decide what to do with it."

"I will speak of it to David when the time comes, Abba, but he is occupied with securing the rest of Israel at the moment." She smiled brightly at her father. "Besides, I do not expect to have to deal with that for a long time to come."

The sun began its descent, and Abigail rose. "It is time for the evening meal. David honors the Sabbath when he is here, even though some of his wives are not Hebrew. Come, let us prepare ourselves."

With David gone to visit some dignitary or other, her father was willing to say the prescribed prayers. They celebrated in the stone dining area they used for meals. Ahinoam joined them for the meal and seemed pleased to meet Abigail's father. She had not seen her own parents since becoming David's wife.

David was able to join them on the third Sabbath of her father's visit and greeted him respectfully.

"It is good to finally meet the father of Abigail."

"Thank you, your majesty. And I at last am able to meet her husband. May I extend my blessings to you on your ascension to the throne."

"I am honored to have your blessing." He looked over at Abigail. "Your daughter has presented me with a fine son. She has been a worthy wife."

Abigail bowed her head at David's praise, but inside, she burned. Was she worthy only because she had produced a son?

Ahinoam brought Amnon to see his father also, but the boy was unruly and made it plain that he was bored with all the people talking and not paying attention to him. He became disruptive and with a glance at Channah from Ahinoam, he was quickly taken from the room.

David had looked after him, a frown upon his face, and then he directed a deliberate look at Ahinoam. Her face reddened with shame. Having been chastised by the look from David, Ahinoam rose and excused herself, and quickly followed her son from the room.

To Abigail's delight, David put Chileab on his lap and let the little boy play with his beard. His babbling made David laugh, and it warmed her heart. Finally, Abigail excused herself and, along with Talia, took Chileab upstairs to bed.

Her father remained and as she walked away, she heard the murmur of their voices.

Ahinoam did not bring Amnon to the garden again while Abigail's father was there, and Abigail felt she was still feeling the sting of David's silent rebuke. Chileab delighted in showing his grandfather all his special places in the garden. There were bugs and other small creatures to examine, the lizard that perched on a rock watching them and puffing its chest in and out, butterflies that fluttered over the flowers. The nest a bird had made in the olive tree absorbed them for many hours. All were exclaimed over and discussed solemnly.

Abigail delighted in watching the little boy and the old man, absorbed in what they were doing together. She listened to the chuckle of her father mingled with the childish giggle of her son and was more content than she had been in a long time.

When it came time for her father to leave, Abigail struggled with a sense of loss. Would she see him again? She watched him walk through the garden with Chileab and held back tears. Her father seemed so vital and strong, but if he died, what would she do? Would David allow her and Chileab to go home to mourn him?

Would he insist that his son remain in the palace? She watched her father ride off and turned away, still another ache in her heart. Seeking the quiet of the garden, in a place where her servants knew not to disturb her, she poured out her heart to her God.

CHAPTER TWENTY-FOUR

When Abigail entered David's chambers one stormy afternoon nearly three years later, she was not surprised to find him hunched over his desk, scrolls and parchments scattered around him. This had become a familiar scene through the years. David never summoned her when his advisors were around, and she was not sure if they knew that her counsel was often behind her husband's wise words and decrees. He had come to trust her shrewd judgment when it came to building his kingdom. She took a seat on the wooden chair across from him, as had become their routine, and he handed her a note inked on heavy parchment. It had been creased many times, and it was stained, as if carried a long distance.

"What is this?"

"Read it."

Abigail was the only one of his wives who could read, a fact that David admitted delighted him. She looked down at the parchment.

Doesn't the entire land belong to you? Make a solemn pact with me, and I will help turn over all of Israel to you.

It was signed with Abner's seal.

"Is this a trick?"

"I do not believe so."

"Why would he do this?" Abner was the real power behind Saul's son Ish-Bosheth, who still claimed the throne of the northern parts of the kingdom. For the past seven and a half years, Abner and the house of Saul had fought against David, trying to lay claim to the southern lands of Judah. Why would he relent now, after so many pointless battles, and take his backing from Saul's son? "Why would he finally acknowledge that the land has always been yours to rule?"

A smile crossed David's face, and he let out a laugh. "I am told that there is trouble between Abner and Ish-Bosheth. It was started, as most troubles often do, because of a woman."

There was a look of tenderness on his face. David had certainly faced plenty of trouble with women, she could attest. He loved pretty women—he always had—and his six wives had done more than their share of fighting and jockeying for position. Abigail had managed to mostly stay above the fray—another reason David valued her.

"What has this poor woman ended up in the middle of?"

"I had a feeling you would take the woman's side."

"It is always the fault of the men."

They smiled at each other. The passion of their early years had cooled to a sense of respect and understanding, and Abigail knew she was lucky in that sense. David never called on Ahinoam at all, and largely ignored her except as it related to the crown prince. Abigail knew she should be grateful for the turns their relationship had taken, unusual as they were.

"It seems that Abner took up with one of King Saul's concubines," David said.

"Why do men never learn?" Abigail had known it had to be something of the sort. "Ish-Bosheth did not take the news well?"

"It appears it is not just his father's throne that he lays claim to," David said.

"I see." Really, men acted like children sometimes. With the fate of the nations resting with them, why would they squabble over a concubine? "And so Abner is out of favor."

"It appears so. So now he has promised to deliver Ish-Bosheth's lands to us. And he sent this." He gestured toward the note.

"You will meet with him, of course." It was not a question. This was what David had been working toward for so long. It was what the Lord had promised so many years ago.

"I wanted to make sure you agree that it is wise."

"What do your advisors say?"

"Joab thinks it is a trick, that he will come to spy. But Abner killed Joab's brother Asahel in battle, so his judgment is probably clouded. Ishbaal thinks we should be cautious but meet with him. Eleazar is convinced he wants to rob us."

"Which of them do you believe?"

"I am not asking them." The candle on the table threw moving shadows across his face. "I am asking you."

"I think you would be a fool not to meet with him. At least see what he has to say for himself."

A smile spread across David's face. "That is what I thought you would say. I will send a message back now."

It was not until many weeks later that Abigail learned that David had written more than his agreement to meet in his note back to Abner. He had also made a demand of his own, as she soon learned.

Abigail was looking out her window onto the courtyard when Abner and his men rode up to the palace. She had prayed that truly Abner meant peace with David and that this was not a trick. She watched the riders dismount and then looked closer. There was a woman with them. She was very beautiful, her hair twisted up in a carefully arranged style, her figure slim, her clothes fine. But she was not young, and her face bore a scowl. Who was she?

The palace knew that Abner and his men were coming. There had been no mention of a woman.

Talia came to the window and looked down with her. "She is here, mistress."

"Who is she?"

Talia looked at her. "You have not heard, mistress? It is Michal, the first wife of our king."

Abigail felt fear clench her heart. He had asked for Michal back, and Abner had brought her. Why had he asked for her? After she had been taken away from David, Michal had been married again. Was her husband dead, or had Abner just taken her away from her present husband as she had been taken from David? Why did he want her, when he already had six wives? A hundred questions played through her head, but she had no answers.

Abigail needed to learn more. She came away from the window and made her way to the balcony that overlooked the great hall. The room had been expanded over the years, and was now grand enough for a king. Abigail stood in the shadows, listening. Ahinoam soon joined her, no doubt drawn by the same curiosity that had brought Abigail here.

Beneath them, David sat on his throne, leaning forward as he watched Abner and his entourage enter the hall. Abner bowed to David. "I have complied with your wishes. Here is your wife, Michal."

Abigail could see now that she was tall, her figure lithe. But her face was stoic, unreadable, as she bowed low before David. "My lord."

"She is quite pretty, isn't she?" Ahinoam whispered. Abigail nodded.

"Michal. I have missed you." David stepped down and approached her. He looked her over, and his face registered pleasure. Pleasure, and something more.

"He loved her," Ahinoam said quietly. "I can see that now."

"I think you are right," Abigail said, seeing the naked hope on her husband's face.

But Michal did not betray the same emotion. Michal stood before him, but in her face Abigail could see no welcome.

David clenched his jaw. "I am glad to finally have you with me, where you belong."

She did not respond, and she did not meet his eye. David grew frustrated. He was not used to being ignored, especially in front of so many people. He gestured to a servant nearby. "Escort my wife to her new quarters." His voice had an edge to it. "I will speak with you later, Michal."

David was not pleased, that much was clear. He had expected Michal to be grateful she was with him once again, Abigail suspected. Any man would, but especially one who was used to women falling over themselves to be with him. Especially a king.

Michal did not look at him as she walked away. She kept her chin raised, her steps languid. Still, he watched her as she walked all the way across the room and out the door. Abigail felt sure he would be calling for her tonight.

Abigail turned to Ahinoam. "She is his first wife, but even if she produces a son, you have given him his firstborn. Take comfort in that, Ahinoam."

"Thank you, Abigail. That was kind." She sighed. "I wonder how many more wives our king needs."

Abigail wondered the same thing.

CHAPTER TWENTY-FIVE

❖

A great feast was prepared for Abner and his men. David wanted to celebrate his coming rise to the throne over all Israel. A fatted calf had been roasted and was served with saffron millet with raisins and walnuts, goat cheese with olives and melon, pomegranate, and poached apricots in honey syrup, and large bowls of grapes.

The men ate heartily, and the servants made sure every man's wine goblet was kept full.

The next morning, the men gathered in David's quarters to discuss the reason they had made the journey. Abigail was stunned to be summoned to join them. When Nour ushered her into the room, she hovered in the doorway, unsure why she was there.

"Abigail. Come join us," David said, gesturing for the men to move to allow her to join them around the table. None of the men moved. Neither did she.

"Come on." He turned to the men. "My wife is very wise, and she gives me advice I rely on. I want her perspective on these negotiations."

Again, none of the men moved. None of them had ever heard of a man asking his wife for advice in private, Abigail knew, let alone seating her at the table with the most important advisors in the kingdom. No doubt they were all wondering whether David had lost his mind. She was starting to wonder the same thing.

"My lord," Eleazar started. If David would listen to arguments from anyone, it would be him. "Do you not think—"

"I think you need to make space for my wife, as I have already directed."

For a moment, still no one moved. Then, reluctantly, slowly, Joab and one of Abner's men moved their chairs, just a bit, and one of the servants brought another chair from somewhere and set it at the table. No one seemed sure what to do. Abigail stood frozen. It was one thing to offer David advice privately, but this was asking too much. She was not qualified to sit at this table. Women were not allowed to do such things.

"Come, Abigail." David's voice was easy, as if he could see nothing irregular with this situation. "We cannot start until you sit down."

Abigail did not know what else to do, so she pushed down the fear that gripped her and slowly made her way across the floor and lowered herself into the chair. Joab and the Israelite man scooted their chairs farther away. She had never been seated so close to men before. She was not even sure this was allowed.

Then again, David was the king. He made the rules about what was allowed and what was not. And he had clearly decided he wanted Abigail at the table with him.

"Now," he said, turning back to Abner. "Tell us why you have come."

"It is just as I said, my lord, in the message I sent to you." Abner had loomed as such a big figure in the minds of David's advisors over these past seven years, and Abigail was surprised to see that he was a small man, with graying unkempt hair and beard. He had scars on his cheeks from spots when he was younger, and his teeth were yellowed and crooked. "I want to make a deal to deliver the kingdom of Israel into your hands."

"You were behind Ish-Bosheth's claim to the throne in the first place," David said calmly. "And you have led Saul's armies against my own for the past seven years. You have done everything in your power to keep me from taking over as king of all of Israel, as the Lord promised. And now you have come to deliver it into my hands?"

"Yes, my lord."

"What is the reason for your change of heart?"

"I have come to recognize that Saul's son is not fit to rule."

"Because of your disagreement over his concubine."

"His *father's* concubine," Abner clarified. The men around the table tittered. "She was Saul's favorite, and I came to understand why."

The men around the table now laughed, and one of Abner's men made an obscene gesture. A few of David's men glanced at Abigail nervously and then looked down.

"I did not realize that Ish-Bosheth also enjoyed her services," Abner continued. "And his rage was well beyond what was reasonable. I came to see that he was nothing more than a child, after all, claiming all the toys as his own."

"You have abandoned your king over a woman." David's eyebrows were raised.

"Not simply over a woman. That was simply what finally caused me to confront what I had known for some time but refused to acknowledge. Ish-Bosheth is a brute, unthinking, and he does not have the common sense to rule."

"Did you not see that before you installed him as king?"

Abner paused a moment before answering. "He would never have been chosen as king if there had been other choices."

Abigail understood what he was saying. If any of Saul's other sons had survived, he would have installed them over Ish-Bosheth.

"And now you have had a change of heart," David said.

Abner nodded.

"You wish to unite the kingdom under my rule."

Abner nodded again.

"And yet you have fallen out with your king," David said. "You no longer have a position in his house. What makes you believe you have the power to deliver what you have promised?"

"I know how things work in the palace. I can promise you that I can make it so."

David thought for a moment, and then nodded. "Very well. I will discuss the matter with my advisors. I will send for you when I have an answer."

Abner ducked his head, rose, and he and his men were escorted out of the room. Abigail started to rise too, but David gestured for her to sit down again.

Once Abner's men were gone, David turned to his council. His council and Abigail.

"He is a spy, my lord," Joab said. "He is here to see how things work, so he can use them against us in battle."

David nodded, taking in the advisor's opinion. He turned to Eleazar.

"I would urge extreme caution," Eleazar said. "I do not know if he is a spy, but I do not trust that after all he has done to keep Saul's son in power he has finally turned his back on him over a woman."

The other men offered their opinions, mostly variations on this same sentiment, though one man, Shammah, suggested that Abner might be here in good faith but couldn't actually deliver what he had promised.

Finally, David turned to Abigail. "What did you think?"

She felt all their eyes on her. Abigail took in a deep breath, hoping to calm her racing heart.

"I believe he is earnest," she said. It came out more quietly than she had intended.

"What was that?" David was leaning in.

She cleared her throat and tried again. "I said, I think he is earnest. I believed him."

For a moment, no one spoke. The men around her were unsure how to respond.

"Thank you." David then sent them all out so he could pray and seek the Lord's counsel. Abigail felt the men's eyes on her as she made her way down the hallways. It seemed none of them could quite believe what had just taken place.

After Abner and his men left, David summoned his counselors and Abigail back, and he announced that he had struck a treaty with Abner to build a united Israel.

The men tried their best to show pleasure, but Abigail saw on the faces of several that they could not believe what David had done. David, however, was beaming, strutting around the room, and Abigail could not help feel pleasure that he had listened to her counsel.

"You may go now," he said, gesturing toward the door. But as Abigail started to follow the men toward the door, he called out, "Wait, Abigail. You stay."

Several of the men said things under her breath that she could not hear, but they went out the door. She turned back to David. He had a wide smile on his face, and there was something in his gaze that she hadn't seen in a long time.

"You are soon to be a queen of a united Israel." David cocked his eyebrow.

"And you, my lord, are to be king." She stepped closer, uncertain. "Just as the Lord promised."

"Come closer, Abigail." She moved closer to him, and he pulled her to him. She felt the heat of his body against hers, and it awakened something in her. He bent his neck and kissed her, gently, first on the lips, and then on her cheek, her throat.

She hadn't been with her husband this way in many years, but she felt herself responding as she had when they were newly married.

"You are more than my queen," he said, his breath hot against her skin. "You are the woman behind my kingdom. You have given me wise counsel, and gentle rebuke." His lips traveled down to her collarbone. "You have seen things I have not. You have understood how powerful men think in ways I did not. You are the one who is responsible for making it all happen as the Lord said it would."

Abigail started to respond, but David moved his mouth back to hers and carried her to his bed, and very soon she could not remember what she wanted to say in the first place. She could not think of anything except how much she loved this man.

CHAPTER TWENTY-SIX

When Abigail woke the next morning, David was gone from the bed. She stretched out her arm, relishing the memory of sleeping, once again, in the arms of the king. She lay on the soft blankets, thanking God for the treaty David had come to, for the way in which he had singled her out, and for the pleasure they had shared the night before. Her cheeks flushed, remembering.

When she finally rose, she was escorted back to her rooms, and she sensed a hushed mood in the palace. No doubt they were all absorbing the news that their king would soon be king over all Israel. Yelena lit the fire under her tub of water, and she took a long bath, soaking in the hot water until her skin was wrinkled. Then she climbed out, wrapped up in a soft cloth to dry, and put on a clean robe embroidered in fine gold thread.

It was not until she went out into the garden with Chileab that she began to understand that something was wrong. The servants were all whispering among themselves, and they kept glancing in the direction of the city gates. Abigail heard the mournful sound of David's harp drifting from the area of his quarters.

"What has happened?" Abigail asked the gathered women.

It was Talia who told Abigail the news. "The king's guest has been killed."

"The king's guest?" Abigail could not have heard that right. "The one who left last night? Abner?"

"The very same." Talia nodded.

"That's impossible." But looking at the faces around her, she saw that it was not. "What happened?"

"The king's general Joab rode out after him and plunged his dagger into him."

"Joab!" He had believed Abner had been here to spy, and she knew Abner had killed his brother Asahel. But how could he have killed the man with whom David had just made a treaty? The treaty that would finally make David king over all Israel?

That afternoon, David called his advisors and those of high position into the great hall. David sat on his throne, while Joab stood in the middle of the room. Abigail stood in the balcony surrounding the hall, watching the proceedings.

"I vow by the Lord that I and my kingdom are innocent of this crime against Abner," David said. His voice rang out across the room, his anger and sadness apparent. "Joab, you have done something terrible. Death is not enough of a punishment for you. I curse your descendants as well. In every generation of your descendants, there will be a man who has open sores or leprosy or who walks with crutches, or dies by the sword or begs for food."

Abigail put her hand on her heart. It was a deadly curse to put on anyone, let alone his top general.

David looked directly at Joab and all who were with him, and ordered them to rend their clothes and mourn for Abner. They all did so, keeping their gazes away from Joab. Joab stood defiantly for a moment and then rent his garment. His face was tight with anger, but he didn't speak. David then dismissed them, saying they would be attending Abner's funeral shortly. Joab was led back to his quarters.

When they had gone and David was alone, he lifted a tortured face to her and she looked back, willing strength into him and courage. He nodded, acknowledging her presence, and then put his head in his hands.

The day of the funeral, David walked behind the procession to the tomb prepared for Abner. David and all the people wept at the tomb. Then David sang a funeral song for Abner, his voice clear and carrying through the crowd.

> Should Abner have died as fools die?
> Your hands were not bound, and
> > your feet were not chained.
> No, you were murdered,
> > the victim of a wicked plot.

David was heartbroken, inconsolable. To have been so close to seeing God's promise be realized, only to have it snatched away in such a foolish act. Most in the palace did not understand why David was so gutted by the death of a man who had spent his career trying to kill him. Indeed, most thought the king should be rejoicing over his general's brave act. But to the few that knew the truth, it was almost too painful to bear. A pall hung over the walls, and everyone spoke quietly.

"He was always moody, even when he was young. It will soon pass," Michal said to anyone who would listen, though none paid her any mind.

David did not call for Abigail. He did not call for any of his wives. He stayed in his room, and the sound of mournful music drifted out. He was starting to give up hope, she knew, that the Lord's promise would be fulfilled.

Just when Abigail thought things could not get any worse, two men showed up at the palace, carrying the head of Ish-Bosheth, the king of Israel. Abigail was horrified when she saw it from her window, hoping it was some kind of trick. What a vile thing to travel with.

The men identified themselves as servants within Saul's household, but declared themselves loyal to David. They were ushered into the great room, and David dragged himself from his quarters onto this throne. His face was dark as a thundercloud.

"My lord, we have brought you the head of Ish-Bosheth, the son of your enemy, Saul, who tried to kill you. We caught him asleep and slew him. Today the Lord has given my lord the king revenge on Saul and his entire family!" The first man had a smile on his face as he spoke. He was sure, Abigail saw, that they would be rewarded for their work.

But David could barely control his anger. "Who are you to kill an innocent man in his sleep?"

Abigail thought back to the man who had ridden into Ziklag expecting a blessing after having helped Saul lean on his sword. David had killed him without a second thought. She feared for these men.

"He is a usurper, lord," the second one said. "You are the one the Lord has chosen to be the one true king of Israel."

"Is it your place to bring that into being?" David asked. His voice got louder as he spoke. "Do you have the authority to decide matters of life and death? Or does that authority belong to the Lord our God?"

Both men were cowering now, sputtering their denial and begging for mercy.

Abigail watched in horror. These men had done wrong, yes. But didn't David do likewise on his raids? Wasn't he guilty of the same thing? Was it different on the field of battle, or when he was serving a king? Wasn't that what these men had been doing too? Abigail, for all the wisdom David imputed to her, did not understand the way her husband did not see his own hypocrisy sometimes.

David turned to his guards nearby. "Kill them."

Abigail fled before the act could be committed. Head down, she walked back to her quarters and went out to the garden to pray. Her heart was heavy with mixed emotions.

David was a warrior. She knew he had raided enemy towns when he served the king of the Philistines. She knew he had risen to Saul's attention in the first place because of his military skill. Her husband had killed many people. She tried not to think about that, but she always knew it. But somehow, seeing him order an execution like that was entirely different. The man she'd seen in that room wasn't the same man who'd been so tender with her just a few nights before. This man was... She could not even think it. He was brutal.

But the thought that gripped her heart, the one that caused tears to spring to her eyes was, would Chileab be raised to do the things David did? Would he be trained to kill like his father? Would he someday march onto the battlefield and run men through with his sword? Would he march into towns and burn them, killing all in his path? It was inconceivable. And yet it was very likely.

She put her head in her hands. How could she reconcile her love for the man with the fierce, bloody warrior and king he had become?

◆

Abigail was walking in the garden the next day when Michal stepped outside. Abigail did not often see her in the garden. She did not often see her at all. Michal had kept to herself and appeared standoffish whenever Abigail saw her. And she no doubt had a right to, Abigail had reasoned. She had been married to David and then torn apart from him and married off to another man. Her father the king was dead, as were all her brothers. Now she had been brought back here, and her first husband had taken six other wives. She had no doubt witnessed the sight of her younger brother's head being carried into David's palace. It was enough to make any woman retreat into herself, and Abigail had tried to give her space. But now, as she sat by herself under an acacia tree, Abigail felt the sense that she should try again. She approached David's first wife. Michal looked up.

"I wondered how you are settling in," Abigail said. "Is there anything you need?"

Michal seemed to not know what to say. She appraised Abigail, perhaps trying to work out whether Abigail was earnest.

"I am fine," Michal said, and looked down.

Abigail knew she could walk away. Michal clearly did not want her here. But Abigail decided she was not going to. She was going to take this opportunity to try to understand this woman, whom David had loved.

"David was pleased to have you return to him," Abigail said.

"He always did like to collect things he found beautiful," Michal said. "And he never did like it when someone else touched his things."

Her voice was bitter, but Abigail tried not to let it discourage her. Michal had known David when he was young. She was the only one who could tell her more about that part of her husband's life.

"You were not pleased to be asked to return to your husband?" Abigail asked. The air was heavy with the perfume of flowers, and bees buzzed lazily.

"He was my husband long ago, and he was taken from me." Michal reached out her hand and plucked a lily from its stem. "I had a new husband and had grown to love him."

Somehow, it had not occurred to Abigail that Michal might have loved the man she had been given to after David. To Abigail, no man would ever compare to David. But Michal had moved on in her heart.

"I am sorry," Abigail said simply. "It could not have been easy to leave in that case."

"It was not my choice." Michal picked a petal off the lily and let it fall to the ground. "It never is, is it? Women are just playthings for the men. What we want does not matter." The petal landed at her feet silently.

It was a cynical way to think about life, but Abigail could not disagree with the truth of her statement. Abigail decided to try another line of questioning.

"Has he changed much?"

"David?"

Abigail nodded.

Michal picked another petal and let it fall. The sweet, heady scent of the lily drifted toward Abigail. "Yes, in some ways. In others, no."

Abigail waited, hoping she would go on.

"He was always the most engaging one in the room. The one everyone wanted to be around," Michal said. "Even when he was just a young musician in my father's court, he gained attention just by walking into the room."

David had a presence you could not help but be drawn to. Apparently it had always been so.

"In that way he is the same." Another petal fell. "And he has always been fearless. Even as a boy, when he was surely too young to be involved in battle, he did not seem to fear it the way many men do. It was like he always knew death would not come for him. Not yet anyway."

Abigail nodded. She had seen this too.

"And he always did have a weakness for pretty women." Michal gave her a wry grin.

"It must have been hard to realize that he had taken many wives after you."

"I was not pleased," Michal said. Something in her countenance softened. "But I cannot say I was surprised. I know him too well for that." She pulled off another petal, but instead of letting it drop, she crushed it with her fist. "He wanted my sister Merab first, you know."

"I did not know."

Michal nodded. "She was the beautiful one. The one every man wanted. David agreed to fight with Saul in order to marry her."

"Why did he not marry her?"

"My father secretly had her married to another man." She let the bruised petal fall. "I was his second choice."

"He has always kept you in his heart. I realized that when he saw you that first day."

"I loved him, once." Michal let out a breath. "I loved him desperately. I actually begged my father to let me marry him once Merab was married to Adrial. I did not realize that my father was already trying to get rid of him because he was fearful of him."

"Is it true he sent David into battle for the right to marry you?" Abigail had heard the rumors of how King Saul had demanded David present him with the foreskins of one hundred Philistines for the right to marry Michal. David was said to have returned with two hundred.

"My father sent him into battle hoping he would be killed," Michal said. "He thought there was no way David could return victorious. But when he marched right back into the palace, cocky as ever, and presented his prize to my father, there was nothing he could do."

"You were pleased?"

"I was. As I said, I loved him." She shrugged. "We were happy together, for a time at least."

"What changed?" Abigail could not believe Michal was talking frankly to her like this, and wanted to keep her talking.

"My father grew more and more unstable. He was threatened by David and feared he would overtake the throne." She laid the flower down next to her on the bench. "It was actually my brother Jonathan who suggested David flee the palace one night, for his own safety. We both believed he would be killed."

"Did you agree?"

"It does not matter what women think, remember?" She gave a sad smile. "But yes, actually I did. I saw the rages my father flew into. When he summoned David that night, I saw the state he was in, and I feared he would kill him. I helped him get away, actually. I hid idols in the bed when my father came looking for him. My father was too drunk to see that it was not David's form under the blanket."

"Why did you not go with him?" This was what Abigail had never understood. Why had Michal not escaped from the palace with her husband? Why had she not stood with him?

"I did not realize how long he would be gone. I thought it was just for one night."

Abigail felt a sense of sadness come over her. Michal had not intended to stay apart from David. But that night had changed everything.

"We soon realized that it was not safe for him to return, and Jonathan urged him to stay away."

"Your father did not take it well?"

Michal let out a bitter laugh. "No, he did not take it well. That was when he declared my marriage to David over, and sent me off to Paltiel."

"I am sorry." Abigail did not know what else to say. Michal had been treated poorly, there was no doubt about it.

"Thank you." She gave Abigail a sad smile. "You are the first one here to be kind to me. Everyone else seems to be afraid of me."

"I believe they are jealous," Abigail said. "I think we could all see that David loves you, and he always has."

Michal gave a small shrug of her shoulders. "What we had once is long gone." She turned and gestured around the garden. "And now I am one of many."

Abigail reached out and touched her arm. "I am glad you are here."

Michal nodded, but she did not say anything, looking off at some point far in the distance.

CHAPTER TWENTY-SEVEN

A few weeks later, the leaders of the remaining tribes of Israel arrived at the palace in Hebron. They had sent a messenger ahead, and David greeted them, sitting on his throne. He was dressed in his finest robes, purple and blue, and richly embroidered with gold thread. The guests made their way across the smooth stone floor of the great room, their eyes cast down. David watched them come, his chin raised, just the hint of a smile on his face.

When the group reached the dais, David pushed himself up and stepped down to meet them.

"Welcome to Hebron. I am honored you have come."

The spokesman bowed low before David. "I am Josiah, and speak for all of us."

Abigail watched the scene from the balcony, along with Ahinoam, Michal, and the other wives. They all knew what this meeting was really about, and they all wanted to see this. Abigail could not help but feel giddy. Fifteen years ago, God had chosen a shepherd boy, and now His promise was coming to fruition. With Ish-Bosheth gone, it was finally time for David to take his throne as the ruler over all Israel.

"We have conferred among ourselves," Josiah continued. "And we have remembered that God anointed you for this. We would like you to become king over all of Israel."

David's face betrayed triumph. "I am honored," he said. "The Lord has fulfilled His word to our people."

Abiathar, David's priest, was called to establish a covenant, and a scribe was sent for to note the occasion. David's other advisors and his military leaders already watched from the floor. Part of her wished she was down there with them, but she knew that would have been too shocking for too many. Instead, she watched from up here with the women.

When the covenant had been witnessed and signed, Abiathar anointed David King of Israel. Then Abiathar brought out the crown, encrusted with jewels, that the Amalekite had brought after killing Saul. As it was placed upon David's head, a cheer went up from all assembled.

A great banquet was ordered for the occasion. Tonight, there would be much rejoicing. In the distance, she could hear trumpets blowing all over the city as the people rejoiced in their king who was no longer just the king of Judah, but the king of all Israel.

David started to walk toward the door of the great hall, and a path cleared before him. The people began to file out behind him. Just as he reached the door, however, David stopped and turned back, gazing up at the balcony. Several of the other wives smiled or waved, likely thinking he was acknowledging them, but as Abigail met his eye, she knew.

She was not surprised when David called for her shortly afterward. The banquet would start shortly, but as the late afternoon's rays lit his chambers with a warm glow, he sat at his desk, studying his maps. He looked up when she entered, and a smile spread across his face.

"Abigail." He stood.

"My lord." She walked toward him, her chin lifted, and, feeling bold, leaned toward him and kissed him. "I wanted to be the first to kiss the new king of Israel."

He did not contradict her, but the guilty look on his face as he pulled back said what he did not. She was not actually the first. One of his other wives had been here before her. No doubt it had been Abital, she thought. David could never seem to get enough of her. This was not that kind of visit then. Abigail tried to put the thought of Abital out of her mind and focus on the present.

"Thank you for coming," David said. She nodded, though they both knew she could not have refused him if she wanted to.

"What do you need, my lord?"

He gestured for her to come over to his table and spread out the map of the area. "I wanted to ask your thoughts on a matter," he said.

She sat down next to him and waited for him to go on.

"Bethlehem," he said simply.

"The city of your birth," she said. "What about it?"

"I am thinking of ruling from there."

"You will not lead your kingdom from here?" Abigail had grown used to this palace, this city. It had not occurred to her that they would move.

"This has been a fine location. But does it not mean something for a king to rule from the place of his birth?"

Abigail had never been to Bethlehem. She was sure it was lovely, up in the hills. It was said to be a thriving city along a much-traveled trade route. But she had heard court gossip that caused her to pause. "Haven't the Philistines taken that city?"

David nodded. "I now have the finest army in the world. I am not concerned about routing out the Philistines."

"You would start your rule with a war?" Wasn't half the point of a united Israel that they would no longer spend all their time fighting?

David sighed. "Ruling is about war, Abigail."

Surely that could not be all it was. Surely there was another way. But instead of answering, she looked down at the maps spread in front of them. She studied the small dots, the thin lines of ink left by the quill. Most of them were just names to her. She knew so little about the world beyond Carmel, Maon, and Hebron. David had been to many of these spots, but she did not know much about any of them.

"What does the Lord say?" she finally asked.

"I am interested in what you have to say."

At her withering glance, he let out a breath. "I have not received a clear answer yet. Though I have been asking," he said.

Abigail studied the lines that showed the boundary of Israel, in the north, and Judah, in the south. The map would have to be redrawn now, she realized.

She narrowed her eyes, looking at one of the dots on the map. She did not know much about it, except that it was a city of Jebusites. But it was on the border of the land that had been Israel and the land that had been Judah. It was neutral, in that way. Neither nation would feel that David had chosen the other. And since it had belonged to neither group, it would rightfully belong to David and his descendants, and neither group could lay claim to it. It was hilly, easily defensible.

It would mean a war, of course. The Jebusites would not give up their city willingly. But David had already demonstrated that he was willing to go to war.

"What is it?" David asked, narrowing his eyes at her.

She hesitated. It was ludicrous that she would make a suggestion like this. Then again, who could ever have imagined she would be here in the first place, married to the king of Israel? Consulted about matters of men? The Lord either had a sense of humor, or He had placed her here for a reason.

A ridiculous thought came into her head. Maybe one day a queen would rule a nation. It was unthinkable. Completely implausible. And yet wouldn't it be amazing?

"What are you thinking?"

Finally, she spoke.

"What about Jerusalem?"

CHAPTER TWENTY-EIGHT

❖

Too soon it seemed, David and his men geared up for battle and marched toward the city of Jerusalem. In the weeks that had followed her impetuous suggestion, David had sent scouts to check out the city, and they found it situated high in the hills, easily defensible from all sides. Abigail had wondered if this might make it challenging for the Israelites to take the city, but David was not worried. The Lord, he said, was on his side. And it appeared it was so. His advisors declared the city suitable, and David readied the Israelite army for battle. Joab, restored to his position one again, led the charge.

As they marched out, Abigail stood with Ahinoam and watched thousands upon thousands of men march in line out of the city gates. Their armor glinted in the sunlight.

Abigail prayed aloud that Yahweh would protect their army and that David would come home safely to her. Ahinoam sniffed next to her. To *them*.

"They will be all right," Abigail said. Ahinoam did not answer, watching the line of men snaking down through the valley.

Couriers rode back to the city a few days later, bringing word of the battle.

"The king is victorious!" they cried. "The king entered the fortified city through the water tunnel, and Jerusalem was taken!"

The entire palace rejoiced in the news. The battle had been short, and all went as David planned. She was glad for him, hoping he would return to Hebron soon.

Instead, though, word came that he had sent for King Hiram of Tyre, who had agreed to provide timber, carpenters, and stonemasons. They were building a palace. The men were working in shifts, day and night, to complete the palace as soon as possible.

Abigail stood on the roof of the king's house in Hebron and looked out toward Jerusalem, that distant city. She pictured David giving orders and inspecting the work. She didn't know how long it would take for the palace to be constructed, but knowing David's impatience to carry out something he wanted, she felt it would not be many months before he sent for his wives and children.

She passed the time in the garden with Chileab, who was now a curious boy of six, or visiting with Ahinoam or Michal, or at her loom. As always, working the soft fibers into beautiful lengths of cloth soothed her.

Finally, word arrived that they were to prepare to make the journey to Jerusalem. The servants packed carts with dresses, bedding, and jewelry, following the orders of their mistresses, and obtaining wagons and other transportation for the wives, concubines, and children, along with provisions needed for the trip. It would be a huge entourage, and David had sent a company of soldiers to accompany them and provide protection on the journey.

The procession stretched out over a mile. Each wife had her belongings and her servants. There were carts for the young children who could not walk. The wives rode on donkeys. Some of the soldiers went before them, and others were interspersed among them to handle problems. Another group of soldiers brought up the rear. The distance was twenty-eight miles, a grueling journey by any measure, and the king's orders were that they were to stop only as necessary. The men would stand guard during the night in shifts.

Abigail wrapped her mantle around her head so only her eyes looked out at the landscape. Chileab wanted to ride in a cart with Amnon, Absalom, and Adonijah, his half brothers. Abigail reluctantly agreed. Tamar, Absalom's sister, rode with her nurse, with her mother on a donkey next to them.

Abigail looked back many times at the cart where Chileab rode to make sure Amnon was not bullying her son. Ahinoam hadn't been happy with the arrangements but reluctantly agreed at Amnon's insistence.

When they came to their stop their first night, Chileab was brought to her. He didn't feel like eating and complained about his head hurting him. She asked if anyone had bothered him, thinking of Amnon, but Chileab said no. She settled him for the night on a pallet and lay down next to him. He was restless through the night, and the next day she took him to ride with her on her own donkey and let him lean against her. He slept from time to time and seemed to find comfort with her arms around him. She rubbed his head and vowed to seek a healing woman when they reached Jerusalem, if there was indeed such a woman there.

The journey was long and hot. At the end of the third day, Jerusalem came in sight, and Abigail was stunned. The city was high on a hill, with thick walls all around that seemed almost iridescent in the light of the setting sun. This would be their new home.

The women murmured among themselves, and Abigail looked back at Ahinoam, who was also looking at the city in amazement.

A small whimper from Chileab brought Abigail's thoughts quickly back to her son. She felt his forehead and realized he was feverish. She motioned to one of the soldiers and explained the situation. He saluted and wheeled his horse to speak to his captain. The captain came immediately and Abigail and Chileab were removed from the caravan and escorted with speed into the city and the palace, Talia and Yelena following.

◆

David waited at the city gates to greet his family, and when he saw Abigail and her escorts riding toward him, he strode toward her.

"Abigail, what is wrong?"

"Chileab is ill, my lord."

David took his son in his arms, and Abigail slipped off her donkey quickly to follow David as he carried Chileab into the new palace on stepped stone with quick strides. She barely took in the stone floors and high walls hung with rich tapestries. She was too worried about her son.

"Send for the physician, immediately!" David ordered.

They hurried to the quarters that David had assigned to Abigail, and with her maidservants following behind her, they entered. Chileab was placed on the large bed. They waited for the physician to arrive. The physician, Abigail was to learn later, was a man by the name of Andras, a Greek who had survived the onslaught of Jerusalem as a slave to the Jebusite king. He had been brought to David, who gave him his freedom if he would remain and serve David. He had agreed. Now, the physician's face was grave as he examined the boy.

David was pacing the room. "What ails the child?"

"I do not know, my king. He says his head hurts, but I find no injury or bruise on it. There is much we do not know about the cause of headaches. Something is wrong, but I cannot determine what it is at this time. I will give him a potion for the fever for now."

Abigail's strength was waning, and she struggled to maintain her composure. She fought tears as she looked up to David.

She had not seen him for almost a year, and now she came to him, spoiling his celebration of the reunion of his family, with a son who was ill.

He saw her fighting back tears and came quickly to take her in his arms. "We shall do all that is possible, Abigail. The physician will remain with him for now, as long as he is needed." He kissed her forehead as he had done many times in the past.

"I must leave you to see to the others. There are the others to settle, and my soldiers to house. I will return as soon as I can to see how he is doing."

She watched him leave, her heart heavy. She welcomed his assurance and his affection, yet how much more would his duties as king occupy his time. He was king of all Israel, a momentous mantle to carry.

All through the night, Andras tended Chileab, checking his breathing and looking into the boy's eyes that were glazed with pain. He prescribed another potion of herbs to deaden the pain, and Yelena followed his instructions to prepare it.

Chileab drank the liquid, almost too weak to protest. Abigail went to her knees beside the bed, praying fervently for his recovery. Over and over, she begged the God Who Heals to let him live.

Ahinoam came to see her, and Abigail welcomed the concern she saw in the other wife's eyes. "I pray for you, that your son will recover soon." She sat down nearby and put a gentle hand on Abigail's shoulder and watched the boy for a while.

In the early hours of the morning, David came and prayed over the boy until the sun rose. When he had gone, she went to Chileab's side again and remained there for days, leaving only for necessary times. Talia and Yelena hovered nearby, making sure she ate to keep up her strength.

Chileab's fever came and went, and at one time he seemed to be getting better. Then his head started hurting him again and he whimpered as Abigail spoke softly and soothingly to him, putting cold cloths on his forehead. Andras checked him from time to time, but again, shook his head. There was nothing more he knew to do.

The boy whimpered again and Abigail tried to give him some of the herbal pain medicine again, but he would not take it. Then he drifted into a deep sleep.

After comforting Abigail, David turned to the physician. "Have you determined what is wrong with my son?"

Andras shook his head. "No, my king. It seems to be something wrong inside his head, and I can do nothing." He looked gravely at Abigail, who had returned to sit beside her son.

"Will he recover?" David asked.

The physician shook his head but didn't say anything. He glanced again at Abigail, who was bending over Chileab, putting another cold cloth on his head.

"I fear not," Andras murmured softly.

David put his head in his hands and then joined Abigail on his knees beside Chileab's bed. His lips moved, and Abigail knew he was praying. She had earnestly sought the Lord for her son, pleading with Him not to take another child away from her.

The servants brought food, but David ordered it taken away again.

Talia brought word. "Mistress, the entire city prays for the king's son."

No one disturbed David and Abigail as they kept watch over their son. Word had gone out to David's men and their families of the boy's illness. Abigail knew they were praying and she was, in a small way, comforted.

Through the night, David and Abigail kept their vigil. The physician put his hand on the boy's forehead and checked his pulse, but his face remained grave.

"There is much we do not know about the workings of the body, my king. I can treat the injuries that are visible to me, but what is invisible is still a mystery."

In the early hours of the morning, Chileab murmured softly, "Imma?"

Abigail had been dozing but was instantly awake and bent over him. "I am here, Chileab."

"—my father?"

"I am here too, my son." David moved to take one of Chileab's cold hands.

Chileab opened his eyes and looked past Abigail. "Do— you see them?" he whispered.

Abigail looked around, seeing nothing. She looked over at David, but he shook his head and gave her a puzzled look.

Chileab closed his eyes and his face took on a peaceful look. He took one last breath and was gone.

"No!" cried David. He lifted Chileab from the bed and gathered him to his heart. Abigail cried out and tore her dress, then slumped to the floor beside the bed. Her cries of anguish echoed through the halls of the palace and even the servants knew. The king's son was dead.

CHAPTER TWENTY-NINE

After the funeral, the city remained in mourning, sharing the grief of their king. Chileab had been buried in a new tomb, reserved for members of the royal family. Abigail's father sent word that while he could not make the journey due to his health, he grieved for his only grandson, and his letter of sympathy was comforting.

Today Abigail walked the garden, restless and weary. An ache remained in her heart like a stone. She thought back to the night after the funeral. David had consoled her in the only way he knew, holding her through the night as she wept.

She sought consolation in silence. She had beseeched her God to heal her son, but it seemed as though heaven was silent also. She felt she had lost the one connection to David. She knew he cared for her, but he was occupied with the affairs of the kingdom and she sensed he would add more wives and concubines, who would give him more sons and daughters. She knew she would bear no more children for David. She knew he would still call for her occasionally, but it would be for her opinion on political matters, not for matters of love.

She sought her quiet place in the garden and looked up to the God who had been her strength all her life. She needed His wisdom and comfort.

One morning, while she was praying in the garden, she looked up to find David standing next to her.

"My lord." She rose to her feet. What was he doing here? He had never before joined her—or any of his wives, as far as she knew—in the garden.

"I am sorry to disturb you, Abigail."

"It is all right." Didn't he understand that he was one of the few whose presence was a comfort? Talia and Yelena had moved away so the king and queen could speak without being overheard.

"I was not sure if I should disturb you. But I have wanted to talk to you for some days. I hope you will forgive the intrusion." In this moment, he seemed less like a warrior and king and more like a young man unsure how to speak to a woman. "You were praying."

"I pray all the time, my lord."

It was the time of year when the air grew colder, and a stiff breeze caused Abigail to pull her robe closer around her.

"What do you pray for?"

"I pray for many things. For you, naturally. For the kingdom of Israel. For peace, and for wisdom." She paused for a moment and then added. "For my father, who grows old."

David nodded. "Please continue to pray for all of these things. Please especially pray for me."

She knew the weight of the kingdom was heavy upon his shoulders. And yet how like him, she thought.

"What did you need, my lord?"

David coughed, and stumbled over his words. "I...I wanted you to see it."

She turned. "To see what?" She heard the sound of voices from inside the palace, but here in the garden, it was peaceful.

"I have wanted to consult you on this many times, but I have not wanted to disturb you in your grief. But now...well, it's happening."

"What is happening?"

"The Ark. It is coming to Jerusalem."

"It—" She stuttered. "What?"

"I am bringing the Ark of the Covenant to Jerusalem. It is just as we always dreamed."

Thoughts flooded her mind so quickly she could not get them out. How was this happening? When? Where would it stand? She thought back to those early days of their marriage, lying together in bed, their limbs tangled, dreaming of the day the Lord's presence would dwell in the kingdom His anointed would build. And now, it was actually happening.

"This is wonderful news." And then, "How?"

"It actually started many months ago, soon after we were settled here. I sent for the Ark to be brought from the house of Abinidab to set it up in this city. I sent a cart, and oxen pulled it most of the way here."

"It was not carried by Levites?" The Law of Moses had strict instructions about how the Ark was to be transported.

"It seemed safer this way," David said, his voice sheepish. Abigail knew it was a mode of transportation he had started using while they had lived among the Philistines. It was just one of the many advances they had learned about while living among their enemies. "But one of the oxen stumbled, and one of the men reached out with his hand to steady it."

Abigail gasped. None but the Levites were to touch the Ark. "What happened?"

"The Lord struck him dead."

Abigail was not surprised, but it was devastating news all the same.

"Who was it?" she asked.

"Uzzah."

She did not know Uzzah, but that did not matter. "I am sorry."

"I have sent his widow five goats and a lamb," David said. She knew that he had tried to make it better in the only way he could. He had a good heart, despite it all.

"So what happened to the Ark after that?" Abigail asked.

"I was not sure it was safe to bring it to Jerusalem after that," David confessed. "I had it sent to the house of Obed-Edom, the Gittite."

Of course it was not safe, she wanted to say. It was the dwelling place of Yahweh, the Lord God of Israel. The God who knows all and sees all, Creator of all that is. Safety was not the point. His glory was. But David had not sent for her to ask for her thoughts at the time, so she kept her counsel now.

"But now you are bringing it to your city. What changed?"

David hesitated. "It was time," he finally said.

Abigail knew that was not the real answer.

"And...?"

David had the good grace to look ashamed. "And Yahweh had blessed Obed-Edom greatly because of the presence of the

Ark," he confessed. "He has acquired much wealth since it has been in his home."

Abigail had known it had to be something of this sort. She loved her husband, but he was predictable.

"And now, you hope the Lord will bless this holy city," she said.

"That is not why I am bringing it here," David said. "I am bringing the Ark to Jerusalem because it is as we always dreamed. This will be the spiritual as well as the political capital of the empire. The Lord has made me king, but the whole kingdom belongs to Him."

Abigail nodded. It would be wonderful to finally have the Lord's presence dwell alongside the king He had raised up.

"Will you build a house for it?"

"Not yet," David said. "But soon."

"When will the Ark arrive?" she asked.

"The men are making their way here now," he said. "They should be here within the hour."

"So soon?" Why had he waited so long to tell her?

"I am going out to meet them now," David said. "I wanted you to be able to watch as it enters."

"Thank you, my lord."

"You will want to stand on the top of the city gates," he said. "We will bring it through the streets and into the throne room of the palace."

She nodded. "I will be waiting."

"I must go," he said, and she noticed, for the first time, that he was wearing a priestly garment. "But you will watch?"

He was not commanding her, she understood. He was asking. He wanted her there. He wanted her to see the dream they had created so many years ago come to fruition. She realized that this man who had captivated her from their first interaction, who had loved her desperately once, still cared about her. It was a comfort.

After David left, Abigail went inside and changed into a purple robe, and then she, along with several of David's other wives, made their way to the lookout on the city gates. Ahinoam stood to one side of her, Michal on the other.

She heard them before she saw them. The sounds of lyres, harps, tambourines, castanets, and cymbals echoed through the streets, punctuated by shouts of joy. The sound grew louder, and then they came into view.

David was leading the parade, followed by Joab and Eleazar and many of David's most trusted men. Behind them were the Levite priests, dressed in ephods, carrying the Ark on their shoulders.

Abigail sucked in a breath at the sight. There it was. The dwelling of the Most High, wending its way toward Jerusalem. She couldn't hold back tears. The most holy object in the world—and it was just there, being led into the palace by her husband.

She had imagined this moment so many times over the years, but she had not known how overcome she would feel to be so close to the presence of Yahweh Himself.

Behind the Ark, hundreds and hundreds of citizens marched, singing and shouting for joy. It was the most jubilant, glorious sight she had seen since she had first gazed on the tiny face of her newborn son. It was also the first moment of hope she had felt since his death. She saw that next to her, Ahinoam also had tears running down her cheeks, though the other wives, especially the non-Hebrew wives, mostly seemed confused. Michal wore a hard look on her face.

They watched as the procession passed through the city gates, and then they hurried back to the palace as the parade wound its way through the city's narrow streets. By the time David led the procession inside the palace and into the throne room, Abigail, Ahinoam, and Michal were standing on the balcony, watching.

David jumped and spun and shouted, clapping his hands as he led them into the great hall. His priestly garment flapped and lifted, exposing his legs, but he did not even seem to notice. Michal made a sound in the back of her throat and turned away, but Abigail could not keep her eyes off him. She had never seen anyone so filled with joy.

The Ark was placed inside a special tent David had had erected for it, and as he shouted with excitement, the priests blew their ram's horns.

It was finally real. He had done it. David was the king of Israel, just as God had promised when he was nothing more than a shepherd boy, and he had finally brought the dwelling of the Most High God to his city.

It was everything they had imagined. Everything they had dreamed up together.

And despite it all—despite all the hurt and the jealousy and the heartbreak, despite all the pain and all the years of difficulty—it had all been worth it to see God's promises come true.

She watched David dancing, given over to delight, mesmerized. And she knew, somewhere deep in her soul, that even with all his faults, even with his greed and his lust and his selfishness, that David loved the Lord with all his heart.

She also knew, in that moment, that God would use this man to change the course of history forever.

And, over it all, she knew that she loved him desperately, and she always would, no matter what happened.

Then, David looked up. Their eyes locked, and she felt it. There was triumph on his face, and he nodded at her, gesturing around the room, and then at the Ark.

He was acknowledging, in the only way he could, her part in bringing this to pass. It would never be acknowledged in any other way, she knew. David's mighty deeds would surely be recorded in books, but the nation of Israel could never know about the woman behind the powerful king. No one would ever believe that many of the celebrated king's greatest victories were engineered by none other than his third wife.

The world would always think of Abigail—if they thought of her at all—as the widow of Nabal, memorable only for his senselessness. They would know her as the mother of one of David's sons, the sickly Chileab, who died before his seventh birthday. She would seem a tragic figure. Just another wife among many. Nothing but a footnote in King David's storied history.

But in that gaze, it was clear that David knew, and that he would never forget, what Abigail had brought to pass.

He knew, even if no one else did, that she too had changed the course of history.

And in that moment—in that brief spark of connection before he looked away—she knew that it had all been worth it.

FACTS BEHIND
the Fiction

✦

House of

- Michal
- Ahinoam
  - Amnon
- Abigail
  - Daniel/Chileab
- Maacah
  - Absalom
  - Tamar
- Haggith
  - Adonijah
- Abital
  - Shephatiah

THE WIVES AND CHILDREN OF KING DAVID

King David had no fewer than eighteen women in his household—wives along with concubines, who were secondary wives of lower status. There may have been dozens more of each. We know that David had at least ten concubines, because that is the number he reportedly left in Jerusalem to take care of the palace when he fled a coup launched by his son Absalom.

Bible writers tell us names of only eight of his wives, most notably Bathsheba; Abigail; and Michal, daughter of King Saul. The other five named wives are Ahinoam, Maacah, Haggith, Abital, and

King David

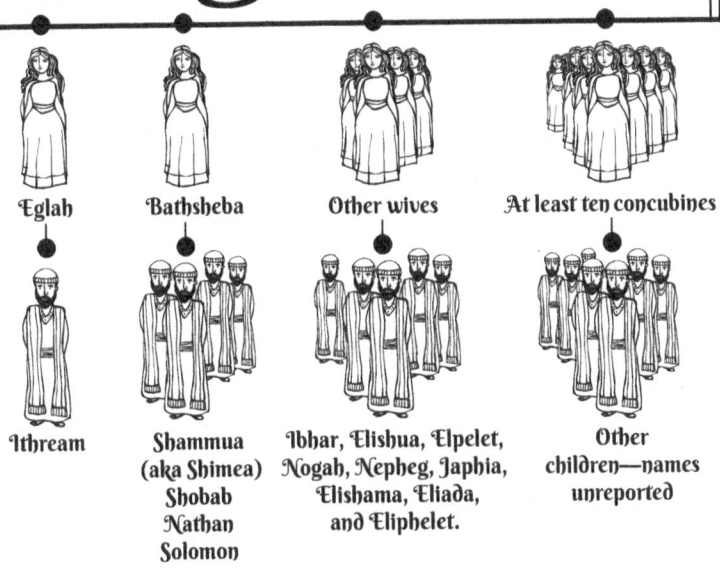

Eglah	Bathsheba	Other wives	At least ten concubines
Ithream	Shammua (aka Shimea) Shobab Nathan Solomon	Ibhar, Elishua, Elpelet, Nogah, Nepheg, Japhia, Elishama, Eliada, and Eliphelet.	Other children—names unreported

Eglah (see 2 Samuel 3:2–5; 1 Chronicles 3:1–3). Michal never had any children because she mocked David for the undignified manner in which he worshipped God as he brought the Ark of the Covenant to the temple (2 Samuel 6), but David's other seven named wives, along with his unnamed wives, produced twenty children. That's "not including his sons born to his concubines" (1 Chronicles 3:9 NLT). And it's not even mentioning any daughters, who were often overlooked in ancient Jewish genealogies.

POLYGAMY: WHY MEN MARRIED MORE THAN ONE WIFE

Men married additional wives because they could. It was a patriarchal time. That's why in the Bible we read about polygamy—men marrying more than one wife, but never polyandry—women marrying more than one husband.

Many of God's chosen leaders practiced polygamy. Abraham, Jacob, Gideon, and Moses all married more than one wife. And scripture tells us that Solomon had a thousand wives.

LEGAL POLYGAMY

One Jewish law allowed for polygamy, as a kind of social safety net. This law surfaces in the case of a married man whose brother dies, leaving a widow childless. Law demanded the surviving brother marry his sister-in-law and try to give her a son, who would become the dead man's legal heir.

If the brother didn't, "elders of the town will then summon him and talk with him. If he still refuses...the widow must walk over to him...and spit in his face" (Deuteronomy 25:8–9 NLT). Then he had to live with a tarnished reputation.

Giving the childless widow a son was important because the woman needed a son to inherit her deceased husband's property. Women usually couldn't inherit anything at all.

POLYGAMY: PERK FOR THE WEALTHY

Polygamy is rare in the Bible, and in scripture it's usually reserved for the rich and influential.

Bible scholars say men married more than one wife for a few reasons, mainly. Sometimes it was simply because they could do so. But also, marriage served as a means of forging alliances between families.

Another practical reason for polygamy: a larger workforce. The family gets more children and more help with work at home and in the fields. If the first wife couldn't have children, or enough children, a man would marry again if he could afford it.

Polygamy was hard on the family—sometimes devastating. In David's family, oldest son Amnon raped his half sister Tamar, daughter of another of David's wives. David did nothing about it except to get angry. Tamar's full-blooded brother, Absalom, got even. He had Amnon assassinated. Later, he launched a coup against his father and died in battle.

David's son with Bathsheba, Solomon, married 700 royal wives and 300 concubines. Many of those women came from foreign kingdoms, even though God warned that marrying outsiders would lead to worshipping gods of outsiders. That's what happened to Solomon, who was otherwise famous for his wisdom: In fact, his wives did turn his heart away from the Lord (1 Kings 11:3–4).

By New Testament times, polygamy became much rarer, and most people had realized life goes better when "a man leaves his father and mother and is joined to his wife, and the two are united into one" (Genesis 2:24 NLT).

A YEAR IN THE LIFE OF A SHEEP

A flock of sheep was like cash in a shepherd's pocket. He could use the sheep anytime to buy products. And, like a pocketful of cash, he could lose the sheep anytime. Shepherds worked constantly to protect their investment from predators, hunger, and thirst.

Winter was lambing time for many ewes, female sheep bred with rams the previous fall. By the time lambs were born five months later, adult sheep had been sheared. Shearing improves the quality of mother's milk—she produces more fat and protein. This is true, in part, because ewes apparently eat more after shearing. A sheared ewe also makes it easier for lambs to find the source of milk.

Spring often turned the countryside green and colorful with grass, flowers, and bushes that sheep eat with gusto. A shepherd with a

A HALF-SHEARED SHEEP

small flock might pay to let his sheep graze with a larger flock, traveling days away for pasture and water. Or he might keep them home and each day walk them to nearby fields. Spring was time to put weight on the sheep.

Shepherds generally let the sheep graze a field just a day or two before moving them on. After farmers harvested crops, such as barley around March and wheat around May, they often let sheep graze on the remaining stubble and dropped grain.

Summertime, often late in the season, became a payday for shepherds who sold sheep for meat and for ritual sacrifices at the Jerusalem Temple. It was also time to breed the best of their flock. Shepherds could earn extra money or add sheep to their flocks by loaning their prized rams to breed with another shepherd's best ewes.

Fall was a time of celebration for shepherds because it was shearing season—the biggest payday of the year. It was at sheepshearing—a working celebration—that King David's son Absalom killed his half brother Amnon while Amnon was "in high spirits from drinking wine" (2 Samuel 13:28 NIV).

When it came time to shear the sheep each autumn, shepherds used shears that looked a bit like hedge trimmers. They would cut each sheep's wool close to the skin so it hung together like a thick cape. Belly wool was the exception. With its shorter wool, more encrusted with twigs and dirt,

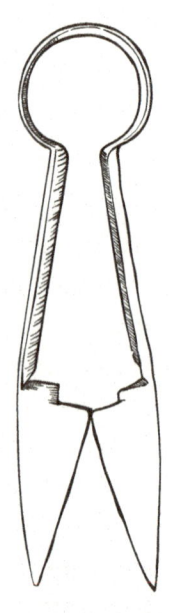

SHEEP SHEARS FROM BIBLE TIMES

300

it may have been set aside as a separate cape, as is often done today. The prize lay in the wool cape taken from the sheep's back, sides, and legs.

Jews wore the wool clothing in David's day. Egyptians seemed to have preferred linen, made from plant fibers spun from woody stems of flax. The Bible cites a law against mixing the two: "Do not wear clothes of wool and linen woven together" (Deuteronomy 22:11 NIV).

SHEARING A SHEEP WITH SHEARS

HOW TO WEAVE ON A LOOM

A weaver needs a loom. Not a big investment in Old Testament times, necessarily. It didn't have to be much more than four small poles tied together as a rectangle, like a doorframe.

The weaver looped strings of fabric, such as yarn, over the top pole and secured them in place with weights—rocks tied to the bottom of each vertical thread, called the "warp."

Next, they needed what's called the "woof," a thread that is woven horizontally, crisscrossing the vertical threads. They did this with a shuttle, which was a bit like a big wooden needle with the woof thread attached to it.

WEAVER'S LOOM

The weaver pulled the threaded shuttle over one vertical thread and under the next, from one side of the loom to the next, and then back again. To speed this up, they added small rods that opened a shaft for the shuttle. Then, after laying down that horizontal thread, they would take a stick that could look like a sword, and they tapped the thread tight against threads woven earlier. They wanted all the threads tightly packed.

Both men and women worked as weavers. In some regions, such as Thyatira, a fabric manufacturing town in what is now Turkey, weavers united to form guilds.

THE NOMAD'S MOBILE HOME

Nomadic shepherds took their homes with them when sheep needed to graze new pasture.

Shepherds, like soldiers on the move, lived in tents. The tents were made from panels of animal skins or from tightly woven black goat hair. Tentmakers sewed the panels together.

Nomads draped the material over poles. Then they anchored it all with strong ropes tied to wooden pegs, which they drove deep into the ground.

When it rained, strands of goat hair swelled and became waterproof. When a panel started showing age, nomads replaced it and then used the aged panel as an inside mat or a wall.

Inside the tent, walls separated males from females. The only males allowed in the women's room were children and the children's father.

In the cold of winter, dark tents retained heat when the sun shone. In the heat of summer, tent fabric breathed, and walls could flip up. This gave the family a well-ventilated island of shade.

The Apostle Paul presented himself as a bivocational minister who paid his own way by making tents. Referring to Paul's work, the term *tentmaker* is often used for missionaries or ministers who work a second job to support their ministry. When Paul spent about three years in what is now Corinth, Greece, starting the church there, he got a job with a husband and wife team of tentmakers, Aquila and Priscilla. They had fled Rome after Emperor Claudius ordered all Jews to leave the capital city.

"Paul went to see Aquila and Priscilla and found out that they were tent makers. Paul was a tent maker too. So he stayed with them, and they worked together" (Acts 18:2-3 CEV).

Paul grew up in a town famous for weaving Cilician goat hair into waterproof cloth for cloaks and tents: Tarsus, in what is now Turkey.

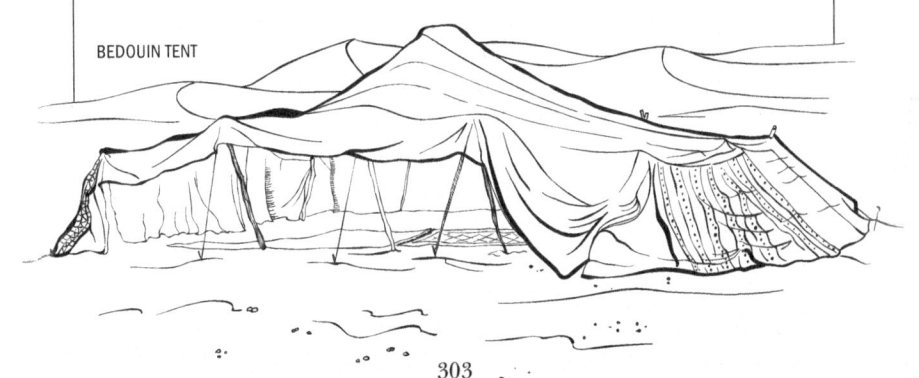

BEDOUIN TENT

Fiction Authors
ELIZABETH ADAMS

Elizabeth (Beth) Adams lives in Brooklyn, New York, with her husband and two young daughters. When she's not writing, she spends her time cleaning up after two devious cats and trying to find time to read mysteries.

DIANA WALLIS TAYLOR

Diana Wallis Taylor lives in San Diego, California, and has been writing since the age of twelve, when she sold her first poem to a church newspaper. Among her fiction projects, she has completed four biblical fiction novels for Revell, with a fifth in progress. She is also the author of three works of contemporary Christian fiction; a poetry book, *Wings of the Wind;* and coauthor of an Easter cantata, *Glorious*. She traveled for many years as a speaker for Stonecroft Ministries and still enjoys speaking and sharing her heart with women of all ages.

Nonfiction Author
STEPHEN M. MILLER

Stephen M. Miller is an award-winning, bestselling Christian author of easy-reading books about the Bible and Christianity. His books have sold over 1.9 million copies and include *The Complete Guide to the Bible*, *Who's Who and Where's Where in the Bible*, and *How to Get Into the Bible*.

Miller lives in the suburbs of Kansas City with his wife, Linda, a registered nurse. They have two married children who live nearby.

Read on for a sneak peek of another exciting story in the Ordinary Women of the Bible series!

AN ETERNAL LOVE: TABITHA'S STORY

by Melanie Dobson

A stone guarded her husband's tomb, the grass around it flattened from his funeral two weeks past. Hundreds had gathered to mourn the loss, but it was just Tabitha now. Alone in this quiet place.

She placed a bouquet of blue and white hyacinths beside the cavern in this olive grove, grief trickling down her cheeks. If only she could dam up her heart with a stone to stop the tears, but nothing seemed to block their flow. Sometimes her tears gushed like waves from the sea and other times they were more like the slow dripping of a water clock, marking every moment without the man she loved.

A *clepsydra*, that's what the Greek called their clocks. Water thieves.

Water had been the thief that stole Isaac from her.

Darkness was falling quickly over this olive grove, casting shadows across the knotted tree roots. Once again time had slipped away for her. She'd lingered too long outside this cavern, as if Isaac's spirit lingered with her. As if returning home meant leaving him behind.

In the distance, she heard a cry. A hyena, she guessed, come to rummage the hilltop dump nearby. At this twilit hour, she'd have to hurry back down to Joppa, to the villa that felt lonelier to her than this grove. To a city fused together by both the Jewish people and Greek.

Olive branches shuddered in the breeze, and the trees looked as if they'd been entranced by the ancient nymphs that were rumored to haunt Judea. She had no interest in mythology about nymphs or Pan—the Greek god of nature—but sometimes these trees seemed just as alive to her as her friends. Walking among them these past weeks, whispering words meant for Isaac alone, didn't stop her tears, but it calmed some of the ache in her heart.

No matter the storm that swept in from the sea, no matter the wicked heat that tormented these trees each spring, they didn't waver. Instead their roots dug deeper into the dusty soil, their arms lifting higher each year in praise to their Creator. In their worship, their branches produced the fruit that gave life to the people in her beloved city, the olive oil providing sustenance and income for their entire region.

How she wanted to be just like these trees, rooted in who God had created her to be, but her roots felt as if they were decaying in the desert winds. She felt as if she might collapse like her mother had once done long ago.

In the past year, Isaac had embraced his new identity as a follower of the Way, a disciple of a man who'd been crucified outside Jerusalem and then, according to Isaac, had walked out of His tomb three days later. The claims this Jesus made, about being both the son of God and man, seemed heretical to her, but Isaac believed these stories. Until his death, she'd faithfully attended the meetings in Joppa with him.

Isaac had always been a good man, but he changed when he decided to follow this Messiah. Not only did he continue his work, he began to give generously of his wealth, like the rabbi named Jesus had commanded those who chose to follow Him, to offer provision to others in need.

She wanted to give of herself, like Isaac had done, but how could she give when the hollow places had seemed to expand inside her, no oil strong enough to heal the wounds of her heart? How could she serve others when she was alone and this Jesus that her husband had decided to follow seemed to steal his life away?

Now her husband's body was wrapped in linen, succumbed to the pain in this world, but if Jesus's teachings were true, Isaac's soul wasn't trapped between the folds of linen in that cave. He was worshipping in the beauty of the heavens, enjoying a palace grander than the one Emperor Tiberius had built.

God, she was certain, loved Isaac. He just didn't seem to love her.

On the other side of the grove, rancid fumes permeated the warmth of the evening, and as Tabitha stepped across a narrow stream and slipped out of the trees, the stench from the city dump burned her nose. She wrapped her black veil, the covering of grief, over her face to block the smell, but it stole right through the silk.

Usually she turned at this crossing, journeying along a path east of here instead of along this ridge, but the setting sun was a daunting opponent. She'd have to circle this dump quickly in order to make it home before nightfall.

She'd soak tonight in a rose-scented bath to cleanse the foulness from her skin, but the smell of decay, she was certain, would plague her mind much longer than her skin, and she didn't want to be reminded of its sorrow.

Life was what she needed. The welcome breeze of sea air below. The refuge of her garden lush with mint and coriander and marjoram. The villa that Isaac had built for a hoard of children who never arrived.

In front of her, vapor sweated off the mount of trash at least two fathoms deep and as long as a fleet of ships. Scavengers sometimes came to the dump at this evening hour, foraging for trinkets among the rubbish, but she didn't see anyone on the hill.

Lifting the seam of her tunic, Tabitha hurried around the perimeter, her eyes focused on Joppa's villas clinging to the hillside below, their lanterns beginning to flicker with light. In the half of an hour, she would be home kneeling beside her bed, begging Adonai to reveal His love. Then she would rest her weary soul.

Another cry pierced the stillness of evening, and her body froze. Hyenas rarely bothered people, but she still didn't want to meet a pack alone at twilight.

Tabitha scanned the rugged slope, the cry growing louder, but it didn't sound like the howl of an animal. It sounded like a baby.

Voices drummed above the sound of cries, two men shouting to each other on the opposite side of the pile. They sounded desperate, as if they must find a treasure buried beneath this trash.

Either scavengers or—

Her heart seemed to stop as she slowly processed what these men might be searching for tonight, the rumors she'd heard of women leaving unwanted—damaged—babies in the dump, as if the boy or girl were garbage.

If the child survived these elements, if a slave hunter found him alive, he would be sold to...

Tabitha shook her head. She didn't want to think about what a child left in this terrible place might be forced to do.

Her hand covered her abdomen, the emptiness of her womb. And she felt the ache anew. How could any woman abandon her baby?

The two men circled to Tabitha's side of the dump, but they ignored her in their quest. Her fear of the men evolved quickly into fear for the baby hidden here.

The lights of Joppa shone brighter, a beacon at the base of this hill, but when Tabitha heard another cry, she turned away from the city, following the sound as she scaled the rotting heap.

Soggy garbage smashed under her sandals, shards of pottery scraped her ankles and toes, but she kept climbing. The men followed closely behind her, but she found the baby first, wrapped loosely in a swaddling cotton cloth, resting inside an old tub. Only hours old, it seemed.

She swept up the child—boy or girl, it didn't matter to her—ignoring the stench of soil on the cloth. The baby's cries settled into a whimper against Tabitha's shoulder.

The men were upon her now, scowling down at Tabitha as if she were a wasp burrowing into their bushel of prized figs. The sun loomed low behind them, its crown flickering the last of its golden blaze before sinking into the sea.

In the fading light, she could see the dirt that stained the men's tunics, the tattered edges of their sleeves, beards tangled instead of trimmed. One of them stepped forward, a braided leather whip secured in his hand. "That's our baby."

Tabitha stood taller, the baby quieting as it nestled close. "Actually, *she's* my child."

While she didn't know its gender, a girl would be less valuable to slave traders than a boy.

"Why did you leave your baby in the dump?" the man demanded.

"I—" Glancing down, she saw the baby's left hand coated in soot. Few in Palestine would want to raise a child—or a slave—with a missing thumb. When the men discovered this defect, they'd probably leave it for dead. "I was going to leave her, but—I suppose I've changed my mind."

"I haven't changed mine." He stepped closer, hatred flickering in his eyes. "And I want that baby."

"It doesn't matter." Tabitha nodded toward the seaport lights. "The courts in Joppa can decide if this child belongs to me or—who are you exactly?"

The men's laughter was wicked, as if she'd made a joke. "We're merchants."

She inched back. "Merchants who know well how to buy and sell, I suppose."

"We're masters at our work."

The trader snapped his whip, and Tabitha cringed as she began backing down the messy slope, begging Adonai to keep these hunters at bay.

The whip snapped again, the tip stinging her arm, and the baby flinched, the cry from its lungs a sorrowful plea.

Anger swelled inside her as she turned back toward the men. How dare they try to hurt a baby who only wanted, *needed*, to be held. A hundred words flooded into her mind, but she dammed them up inside her lest they flood off her tongue.

If she pretended to play the hunters' game, she might still be able to rescue this child.

"Perhaps you can have her after all," she finally said.

The smile that played on the man's lips sickened her. "I'm glad you've come to understand our terms."

"Indeed." Tabitha looked down at the baby again, disdain forced upon her lips before she spoke again. "I suppose, as men who have seen the world, you would understand what to do about her condition more than I."

"What condition?"

She tilted her head, her nose crinkled. "Did you not know?"

When he didn't respond, she eased back the edge of the cotton, revealing the tiny arm of the newborn. The man with the whip stayed at the top of the pile, almost knee deep in trash, but his partner stepped down to examine the baby.

With a gasp, the man's smugness washed away like a boat in one of Joppa's storms. "Leprosy?"

The tears salting her cheeks were as real as the ones that had flowed earlier at Isaac's grave. "I want to do what's best for her."

The man backed away quickly, falling into the heap. A string of curses, longer than a dock line, sailed from his lips. Instead of threatening her again, he seemed to be terrified of this baby.

Tabitha held the child out again. "You will take her?"

Instead of replying, both men disappeared over the hump, swallowed by the darkness to their east.

Tabitha wiped away her tears with the back of her hand before turning toward the light. She cradled the baby close to her chest, hurrying back down yet taking care not to fall. If she injured herself, the two of them would have to spend the night in this abysmal mess.

She didn't know how to care for a little one, but the Messiah, in the teachings that she'd heard, made it quite clear that His followers were to love others, especially those considered to be the weakest among them. Surely someone in Joppa's community of disciples would care for this baby, even if she must pay them for their service.

When she stepped into the safety of the city, to the marketplace that had emptied itself until morning, she tore off the filthy cotton strips and scanned the baby's skin for the curse of leprosy passed along from the woman who'd birthed him.

It was a boy, this baby, and—thank God—she found no sores on his lank body. A missing thumb was merely an inconvenience, not a death sentence.

She needed to find a wet nurse this very night to care for him, lest he slip into eternity before dawn. In the morning, she would clothe him in clean linen and search for a woman—a Christ follower with other children—to mother him.